# AWESOME
# FORCES

# AWESOME

## THE NATURAL HAZARDS THAT THREATEN NEW ZEALAND

# FORCES

Edited by Geoff Hicks and Hamish Campbell

Te Papa Press
Wellington
Published in association with
EQC and IGNS

Te Papa Press
Museum of New Zealand Te Papa Tongarewa

First published 1998
Reprinted with corrections 1999
Text © Museum of New Zealand 1998
Photographs reproduced with permission of the copyright owners

TE PAPA™ is a trademark of the Museum of New Zealand Te Papa Tongarewa
Te Papa Press is an imprint of the Museum of New Zealand Te Papa Tongarewa

Cover photograph of Mount Ruapehu erupting
by Tim Whittaker
reproduced with the permission of the *Hawke's Bay Herald-Tribune*

ISBN 0-909010-58-7

Edited by Anne French
Designed by Nikolas Andrew, A Design
Layout by Shelley Watson
Digital imaging by Jeremy Glyde
First printed in New Zealand by Lithoprint
Reprinted in Hong Kong by Condor Production Ltd.

Published by the Museum of New Zealand Te Papa Tongarewa,
PO Box 467, Wellington
in association with
the Institute of Geological and Nuclear Sciences Ltd,
PO Box 31-312, Lower Hutt
and the Earthquake Commission,
PO Box 311, Wellington

# Contents

# Acknowledgements

Every book project has its unsung heroes. The editors are grateful for the help of the following people, who supplied data, checked details, provided photographs, and occasionally tempered our enthusiasm by providing detailed comments on draft chapters: Chris Adams, Brent Alloway, John Beavan, John Begg, Kelvin Berryman, Carol Bryan, Doug and Ann Campbell, Catherine Chague-Goff, Roger Cooper, Gaye Downes, Atherlie Dreadon, Rodney Grapes, Lloyd Homer, Dinah Riley, Brad Scott, Rupert Sutherland, Kathryn Staples, and Terry Webb. Designer Shelley Watson turned our rough pencil sketches into crisp diagrams. At Te Papa, Alastair McLean beavered over the picture research and Jeremy Glyde painstakingly scanned the images. Jo Martin at EQC provided us with information. Lynley Cunningham of Te Papa and Robin Falconer of the Institute of Geological and Nuclear Sciences provided practical support, making it all possible.

Our thanks to all of you.

Geoff Hicks and Hamish Campbell
*September, 1998*

# Foreword

New Zealand's landscape is one of the most spectacular and picturesque in the world, justly acclaimed by tourists from all over the world and New Zealanders alike. Yet how aware are we of the forces that produced our magnificent lakes, mountains, and rugged coasts? And what happens when these same forces collide with the people who live here?

The North Island boasts one of the most active and most violent volcanoes in the world, Taupo. To most of us it seems nothing but a beautiful and tranquil lake. Who would think that beneath those gentle waters is a giant's cauldron gathering steam for a future explosive eruption? And then there are all the other volcanoes to worry about: Ruapehu, Okataina, Taranaki...

New Zealand is also famous for its earthquakes. We have on average 17,000 earthquakes each year. Six of them are greater than magnitude 6, which means they are big enough to cause major destruction should they strike a city or town. And we are surrounded by ocean, posing an ever-present threat to people living on the coast from earthquake-associated tidal surges or tsunami.

These frightening earth hazards are a symptom of New Zealand's unique place on the Earth's surface. Our mountains too, including the majestic Southern Alps, owe their loftiness to the creeping, sliding, cracking, and crunching processes going on right now, deep beneath our feet. Add to this the curious interaction between these steep slopes and a climate that dumps a lot of water on them, and we have a formula for collapse – landslides. New Zealand has some of the largest documented landslides known, as well as some of the most dramatic.

Our climate and localised weather are part of what has created the character of New Zealanders. They have come to live with its changeability and its potential for untimely suddenness; and in turn they have developed great personal adaptability.

'Live dangerously: take risks!' You don't have to try very hard in New Zealand. The Long White Cloud of Aotearoa shrouds a dynamic, ever-changing landmass that suffers from an unusually favourable disposition to predictably unpredictable natural disasters. Why is this so? What forces are responsible for the way New Zealand is? How dangerous are they? Are they unique to New Zealand? And how do they affect the people who live here?

This book addresses all these questions and provides some answers – not always very comforting! It is a companion to the Awesome Forces exhibition at Te Papa, the Museum of New Zealand. The five major categories of non-biological natural hazard that face New Zealand are covered: volcanism, earthquakes, tsunami, landslides, and adverse weather.

All New Zealanders will face at least one of these dramatic hazards during their lifetime, just by virtue of living in this particular place. All the hazards have two things in common. They involve rapid, large-scale movement or displacement of solids, liquids, and gases; and curiously, they are all noisy! They are all explained with authority and integrity, as might be expected of some of New Zealand's leading scientists. Hamish Campbell sets the scene by considering New Zealand's place on the globe, then follow chapters by Bruce Houghton on volcanism, Alan Hull on earthquakes, Mauri and Eileen McSaveney on landslides, Willem de Lange on tsunami, and Jim Salinger on adverse weather and climate change.

It gives us great pleasure to commend this informative, well-written, and exciting book to all those who live here or visit New Zealand.

The Awesome Forces exhibition and this book are supported by the Institute of Geological and Nuclear Sciences Limited and the Earthquake Commission.

Cheryll Sotheran          Andrew West          David Middleton

*Institute of*
**GEOLOGICAL
& NUCLEAR
SCIENCES**
*Limited*

# Our place

HAMISH CAMPBELL

Opposite: *Planet Earth as seen from space.*
(NASA)

We spend most of our lives lulled into a false sense of security. Volcanoes erupt, tsunami sweep all before them, earthquakes flatten whole cities... somewhere else on the planet. Yet New Zealand is particularly vulnerable. All of the natural hazards described in this book can have an effect on our daily lives. Many of us have encountered several of them already.

The problem is, there's nowhere to run to. Retreat from the eastern coast to avoid tsunami, and you enter the shaky, earthquake-prone mountain ranges. Wellingtonians moving to Auckland before the Big One strikes should beware new volcanoes. You can put the active volcanoes behind you and head south, but whatever you do, watch out for landslides! And no matter where you are, New Zealand's rapidly changing weather will always make its presence felt.

Perched on the collision zone between two gigantic chunks of the Earth's crust, New Zealand has been created by huge forces that continue to shape it. It's a dynamic and dangerous place to live. The big earth processes that created this landmass did so long before humans walked on the planet, and they will continue long after we have ceased to be.

Of all the awesome forces associated with Planet Earth, gravity is the one we most take for granted. Yet gravity holds our planet together, keeps it in position within the solar system, and keeps us on its surface. Without it we'd all spin off into the blackness of space!

For the purposes of this book, we assume that gravity on Earth is an implicitly constant and invariable force and all processes described here are subject to it. Gravity plays a central role as an unseen, silent, awesome force in all natural hazards. Rain falls, land slides, volcanic debris crashes to earth, seismic events flatten buildings. Each is the inevitable consequence of a gravitational Earth.

Heat exchange and temperature variation are additional silent forces that drive almost all movement on this planet. Without gravity and heat, there is no movement.

Gravitational forces are constantly at work pulling all matter toward the centre of the Earth. The rock becomes denser and denser the closer to the centre it is. This gradient in density, coupled with the hot, viscous nature of the mantle (like toffee), are the basis of the convection mechanism that is thought to drive the movement of the plates that make up the Earth's crust, including plate collision. 'Plate tectonics' is a holistic theory that explains the surface motions on the exterior of the planet. The crust could be described as just a manifestation of the interface between the mantle and space. Most of the planet is mantle, and the crust is only its thin skin.

Between 90 and nearly 3000 kilometres below our feet, the mantle is in

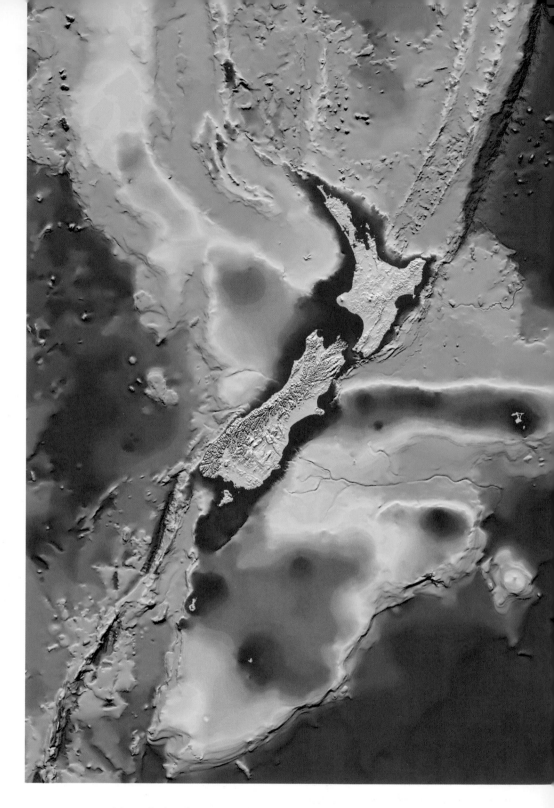

*The New Zealand landmass as it would appear if the sea were removed. This spectacular map shows the submarine topography of the New Zealand region in all its glory, revealing many major features: the broad extent of our continental shelves, volcanoes, trenches and submarine 'river valleys' that run down to the deep ocean floor. It also reveals how little of the New Zealand 'continent' is above sea-level. Were it not for the tectonic forces associated with the plate boundary zone running through New Zealand, there would perhaps be no land at all. Because the Earth's crust is unusually thin beneath New Zealand, its natural level with respect to the surface of the planet is about one kilometre beneath the sea! Conversely, if the crust were thicker, the New Zealand landmass would sit higher and there would be much more land.*

(NIWA)

motion. Heated largely by friction and energy coming up from the core, the rocks of the mantle can reach 4500°C. Just as toffee flows when it's hot, these rocks swirl and creep. At the surface, the movement of the crustal plates is driven by a similar slow convective heat flow process below the crust, within the mantle.

The theory of plate tectonics implies that the crust is mobile. It is this moving and changing over long periods of time that has been responsible for the genesis of New Zealand, and provides an explanation for its particular position on the surface of the Earth.

# The geological setting of New Zealand

The crust is arranged into a number of gigantic rigid slabs of rock or 'plates' (as in plates of armour) which are all moving and jostling at varying rates and in varying directions with respect to each other. The edges or boundaries of these plates are surprisingly well defined. The Earth's surface can be described in terms of 15 major plates. New Zealand straddles the boundary between two of them. It sits on part of the eastern edge of the Australian Plate and the western edge of the Pacific Plate.

So, what did New Zealand look like originally? Where did it come from? Well, the oldest fossils in New Zealand are trilobites of early Middle Cambrian age (508 million years ago). They are found in limestone rocks from Cobb Valley in north-west Nelson. The oldest rocks in New Zealand are volcanic rocks, also from Cobb Valley, that are thought to be 530-540 million years old.

At that time, New Zealand was a small part of the south-east Australian segment of eastern Gondwanaland. This super-continent was enormous, consisting of Antarctica, Africa, Australia, South America, India, and New Zealand, all rolled into one! It could be said that New Zealand has always been on the edge of eastern Gondwanaland... for about 400 million years, anyway. The rocks that make up New Zealand today are largely derived from the erosion of part of the Australian segment of the Gondwanaland super-continent, and accumulated initially as sediments and lavas deposited in the seas adjacent to the great landmass.

Gondwanaland began to break apart about 160 million years ago. By 120 million years ago, South America, Africa, and India had separated. 'New Zealand' was land, but still part of Gondwanaland. Ninety million years ago it was New Zealand's turn to leave home. It was launched as an independent but small continent by a gigantic split along the margin of eastern Gondwanaland. Australia was the last to break free, leaving Antarctica as it is today.

By 55 million years ago, the sea floor between Antarctica, Australia, and New Zealand had stopped opening up, and New Zealand was completely isolated. Over the next 30 million years, the crust beneath the New Zealand continent grew thinner, and it sank lower and lower beneath the sea. Then, about 25 million years ago, the active boundary between the Pacific and Australian plates developed a new position right through the New Zealand continent. This was good news! Without the forces associated with this plate-boundary collision zone, New Zealand would still be a thin-crusted continent lying beneath the sea. The New Zealand landmass with its elongated shape is a consequence of plate collision along a particular segment of the Pacific-Australian Plate margin.

*The bottom third of a New Zealand trilobite. This handsome specimen is 10-15 millimetres in diameter and is named Dorypyge sp. It was collected from the oldest fossiliferous rock known in New Zealand, a limestone in the Cobb Valley of Northwest Nelson. It is of Cambrian age and is considered to be about 508 million years old.*

(IGNS)

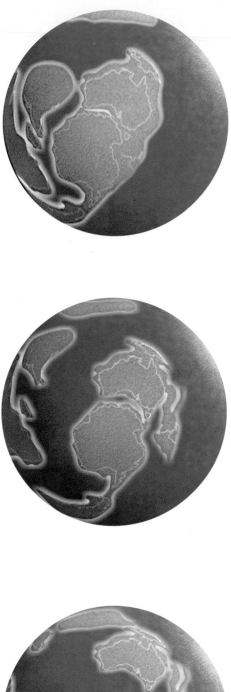

How do we know all this? How can we be so sure? Well, this picture has been built up over many years from careful geological and geophysical mapping, description, and comparisons of strata, rocks, and fossils. Precise measurements of the differences between points fixed to the earth's surface have enabled us to observe the motion of the plates.

Harold Wellman, a surveyor and geologist, was the first person to demonstrate that parts of the New Zealand land surface had changed shape during the years that had elapsed between surveys. This finding was momentous. It completely changed our perception of the world, but like all new ideas of fundamental importance, it took some time to become accepted. Nowadays, with the use of satellite and laser distance measurement technology, extremely precise measurements, sensitive to within millimetres, have become routine.

Over the last few decades, high-tech surveying has enabled us to observe how the surface of the Earth is moving and changing shape. But compared with the rate at which we get about, the movement is imperceptible. The plates move at about the same rate our fingernails and hair grow: about 25 millimetres per year, on average.

It is this relentless plate motion that is responsible for most of New Zealand's hazards, yet it is also responsible for there being a New Zealand in the first place! The shape, position, and relief of our landmass is a consequence or response to plate motion: active volcanoes in the central North Island; the fault-riddled east coast (North Island and top of the South Island); the drowned west coast (North Island), Cook Strait and Marlborough Sounds; the Southern Alps; the Alpine Fault.

## Which plate are you on?

All of the North Island is located on the Australian Plate, and so is everything to the west of the Alpine Fault in the South Island, including Nelson and Westland. The rest of the South Island, Stewart Island, the Chatham Islands and Subantarctic Islands are all on the Pacific Plate. Depending on where we live, this reality might alter our perception of our place of citizenship!

The really interesting bit is the plate boundary: the collision zone. What exactly is happening? Well, it varies, depending where you are.

Off the east coast of the North Island from East Cape to Marlborough, going north-east to south-west, the boundary of the Pacific and Australian plates is marked by subduction where the Pacific Plate dives beneath the Australian Plate. Subduction is the drawing down or

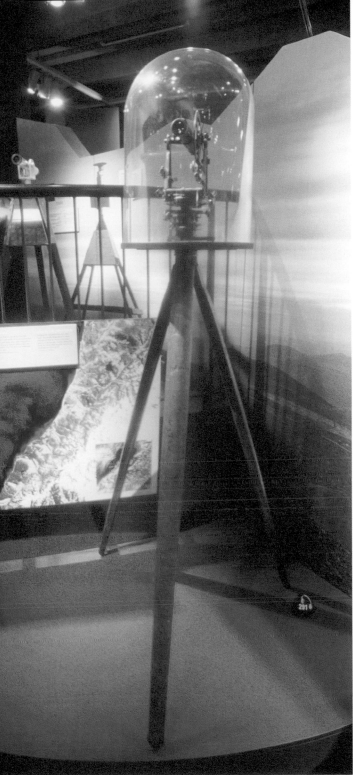

sinking of cold, dense oceanic crust into the hot mantle. This process is a direct consequence of gravity and is most easily recognised and defined by seismicity: a characteristic pattern of earthquakes which denotes the slow relentless passage of a 'down-going slab' at the edge of a plate. As it sinks, it depresses the Earth's surface to produce a 'trench' which normally manifests itself as an elongated, deep submarine depression. The trench associated with the subduction off New Zealand's east coast is called the Hikurangi Trough. As it travels north it becomes the Tonga-Kermadec Trench, up to 10,100 metres. Far to the north-west a similar feature, the Marianas Trench is, at 10,376 metres, the deepest water on the planet.

Subduction is a mechanism that consumes and destroys oceanic crust. It elegantly explains one of the great mysteries of geology this century: why the age of the ocean floors is no older than about 150 million years. Like a conveyer belt, new oceanic crust is produced as lava along the mid-oceanic ridges (which are mostly below water), spreads slowly to the plate margin, and is then subducted. The mid-ocean ridge creating new Pacific Plate oceanic crust runs as a gigantic zipper from California to the southern ocean off Peru and Chile.

The trenches are the 'plug-holes' down which material on the planet's surface is drawn or sucked into the Earth's interior. They are the door to the furnace below, and the primary entry point for that volatile ingredient, water, that distinguishes the volcanoes of the Ring of Fire from all other volcanoes.

Facing page: *Gondwanaland. These three snapshots in time show where New Zealand was with respect to the ancient supercontinent, Gondwanaland, at 120, 55, and 25 million years ago (top, middle and bottom, respectively). Our nearest neighbours have always been Australia and Antarctica. Note that the New Zealand continental fragment splits off before Australia does, and that the Alpine Fault in New Zealand has not moved. It only began to do so about 25 million years ago.*
(IGNS and Te Papa)

Left: *Harold Wellman's theodolite. This is the very instrument with which New Zealand surveyor and geologist Harold Wellman established that the Earth's surface had changed shape as a direct result of earthquake activity and fault movement in the Murchison area of the South Island. These simple measurements led to a fundamental change in understanding of processes operating on the surface of our planet. Wellman's major contribution to science is now embodied in plate tectonic theory.*
(Awesome Forces exhibition, Te Papa)

*Banks Peninsula is the eroded remnant of a large shield volcano of dark basaltic rock. Molten rock erupted from three different centres between 10 and 6 million years ago. The two largest volcanic cones of the peninsula have been breached by the sea, forming the sheltered harbours of Akaroa (centre left) and Lyttelton. New Zealand's second-largest city, Christchurch, is built partly on the volcano's northern flanks. (IGNS)*

## Wet and dry volcanoes

Volcanoes come in two kinds, wet and dry, depending on the amount of water and gas there is in the molten rock or magma. Wet volcanoes are also known as 'explosive', while dry ones are known as 'effusive'. New Zealand is blessed with both kinds, but it is the wet subduction ones that are particularly explosive and dangerous. They may be thought of as giant kettles through which the Earth expels water that has become trapped during subduction. Water, under pressure and very hot, behaves like flux in welding and lowers the melting point of the rock, turning it into a molten, volatile, explosive fluid. The active volcanoes of the Taupo Volcanic Zone are all caused by subduction, all part of the Pacific Ring of Fire, and have all erupted repeatedly. Little wonder that Taupo is billed as one of the world's most dangerous volcanoes.

It is sobering to note that the Taupo Volcanic Zone is continuing to gape open, and is almost certainly moving and growing in a south-west direction, as an inevitable consequence of directional changes in plate motion. This means that in time there will probably be a volcano where Wanganui is now. The city is in a direct line with the Taupo Volcanic Zone and just happens to be the location of most numerous and intense small earthquakes in New Zealand. Geophysicists have been so bold as to name this imminent volcano already!

Mount Taranaki (about 70,000 years old) is also a wet volcano, the product of subduction, but its current location is due to a westward- extending sector of the subduction system. The centre of volcanism is also moving, and Taranaki is the youngest of four eruptive centres in a line south-west of New Plymouth.

Apart from the Taupo Volcanic Zone and Mount Taranaki, the only other area of active or very recently active volcanism in New Zealand is Auckland. Auckland City is literally built on and amongst 48 volcanoes that have all erupted over the last 60,000 years. The youngest, Rangitoto, is only 600 years old.

Like pimples breaking out upon the face of the Auckland landscape, these volcanoes are not related to subduction zones. Instead they have formed well away from the plate margins. These 'intra-plate' or hot-spot volcanoes produce basalt derived from the upper mantle and lower crust. They are dry volcanoes. The magma they produce lacks volatile components, particularly water. Accordingly, they are not nearly as explosive and violent as wet volcanoes. Their magma is more like thick, hot treacle or toffee, and they tend to ooze and flow. Nevertheless, imagine what would happen if an eruption began in suburban Auckland! Volcanism of any description is not a trifling matter and its effects would be devastating.

Christchurch is built to one side of a very large extinct volcano (6-10 million years old) with at least three major eruptive centres that have coalesced to form Banks Peninsula. Dunedin is built within the eroded centre of a similarly extinct composite volcano that is even older (10-15 million years old). A great number of small Auckland-like volcanic centres are scattered through the landscape north and east of Dunedin, towards Palmerston and Ranfurly, the remnants of old mid-plate hot-spots. Oamaru is built adjacent to a small but ancient volcanic centre forming Cape Wanbrow, and Timaru is actually built on the youngest known lava flows in the South Island (less than 3 million years old). Why is it that many of our larger cities are built on volcanoes, silly as it may seem? Volcanoes frequently make big holes in the ground, and when they are breached and fill with water, they make fine deep-water harbours!

Perhaps New Zealand's most spectacular example of a dry Hawaiian-type of shield volcano is the main mass of Chatham Island. This volcano erupted 70-80 million years ago. It has been the locus of Auckland-style 'leaky' basalt volcanism ever since. The youngest eruptive centres are less than 3 million years old (Southeast Island, The Pyramid).

There is one extreme form of dry volcanism that is only sparsely represented in New Zealand: flood basalt

*Chatham Island is the remnant of a very large shield volcano. Similar to those of Banks Peninsula and the Dunedin Volcano, but much older at between 70 and 80 million years (Late Cretaceous), Chatham Island must rate as one of New Zealand's major shield volcanoes. This view is from above Owenga on the south-east coast of the main Chatham Island, looking west along the south coast. Spectacular cliffs reveal a pile of almost flat lying basalt lava that must have flowed northwards from an eruptive centre in Pitt Strait.*
(IGNS)

*A glimpse into the surge zone: elongate, parallel ridges, and range crests are a simple consequence of subduction. Their geometry is telling us not only that subduction is happening, but also where it is happening. The alignment is normal to the direction of subduction. This alignment imparts a grain to the landscape of much of the lower and eastern parts of the North Island. This view is from above Wellington Harbour looking southeast across Mākaro (Ward) Island towards the Orongorongo and Rimutaka Ranges. (IGNS)*

volcanism. Flood basalts pour out in vast volumes in response to major depressurisation events within the Earth's mantle. This situation involves major breaching of the crust. When you take the top off a bottle of fizz, bubbles appear from nowhere. All that has happened is that pressure has been released. Similarly, pressure release in the mantle produces bubbles of molten rock that rise to the surface as lava. A major flood basalt event occurred within Gondwanaland during the Jurassic (135-205 million years ago), and New Zealand has a remnant of some of this rock preserved as Kirwans Dolerite, near Reefton. This constitutes some of the key geological evidence that links New Zealand with Gondwanaland.

While such outpourings are rare, some geologists believe they have the capacity to alter global climate. Two such massive volcanic events occurred at the end of the Permian (250 million years ago) and at the end of the Cretaceous (65 million years ago). Both happened at the same time as mass species extinctions. (At the end of the Cretaceous, it was the dinosaurs that died out.) Could it be more than coincidence? Some geologists think that the flood volcanism may have been caused by the impact of meteorites, and may have led to climate change, which was the ultimate cause of the mass extinctions.

# Our central surge, set in stone

Just like the crest of a great long wave rolling in to shore along a straight beach, so do the ranges of the central North Island rise up, indicating the collision between the Pacific and Australian Plates, forming a series of pressure ridges cast in rock. It is no coincidence that these ranges lie parallel to the Hikurangi Trough, or that they are broadly similar in height. It is all part of the same subduction process.

Ironically, this 'grain' or linearity in the North Island landscape is also the reason why New Zealand can claim to be the land of the long white cloud. The mountains run north-east to south-west, continuing in the South Island as the Southern Alps, and they attract or generate cloud from one end of the country to the other. Even our characteristic weather is a product of subduction at work, with moisture-laden air to the west of the main divide in both islands, drier air to the east.

Why are these mountain ranges here? They are being pushed up from underneath, and are trying to ride up over each other. Just as a rug rucks up when it's pushed against a wall, the mountain ranges reveal the compression within the crust due to plate collision. In the case of the North Island, the eastern edge of the Australian Plate is being squeezed and crumpled by the stronger, heavier, subducting Pacific Plate as it moves westward. This process causes a 'shortening' of the crust at right angles to the subduction margin. In other words, the distance between Napier and Taupo is getting smaller! However, in the South Island the opposite is happening. It is the western edge of the Pacific Plate that is being squeezed and crumpled to form the Southern Alps.

*Large-scale folds can develop within the crust as a consequence of compression (squeezing) and collision near plate margins. Some rocks can be folded more readily than others. For instance, schist folds much more readily than greywacke and this is particularly evident in these Otago mountain ranges. Detailed geological mapping has established that these are huge folds developed within schist!*
(IGNS)

*This diagram demonstrates the simple relationship between the Pacific Plate and Australian Plate in the New Zealand region, and in particular beneath the lower North Island. Subduction of the Pacific Plate beneath the Australian Plate results in a surge of mountain ranges at the leading (eastern) edge of the Australian Plate. The eastern edge is squashed and crumpled, with attendant explosive (wet) volcanism. Further west, a giant sag is produced within the Australian Plate, literally pulled downwards as a result of the descending Pacific Plate. (IGNS)*

Most of this deformation is happening as brittle failure or slippage along faults, but some of the deformation is more plastic and generates folds in the landscape. The best example of such large-scale folding is the basin and range topography developed in the schist country of central Otago. The Maungatua Range, Rock and Pillar Range, Old Man Range, Pisa Range and so on are all thought to be gigantic folds that are still being formed in response to crustal compression operating in a north-east to south-west direction.

The elongated surge zone of mountain ranges in the central part of the North Island is less than 100 kilometres wide, and is the source of many of New Zealand's earthquakes. But further west, a completely different process is taking place. The crust is being dragged down as part of a gigantic sag.

## The big sag out west

As the subducted Pacific Plate continues to grind its way beneath the Australian Plate, it slowly extends deeper down. At depths of 30-35 kilometres, it is well beyond the zone where water is driven off, producing 'wet' subduction-related volcanoes, and well beyond the mountainous surge zone developed in the leading edge of the Australian Plate. However, the Pacific Plate continues to exert an influence on the surface. It quite literally sucks the crust down to produce a huge sag or warp.

It is this phenomenon that explains the long, straight sections of the west coast of the lower North Island, running parallel to the subduction zone. But it explains much more! It indicates why all the rocks in the Wanganui-Taranaki areas are tilting into the Tasman Sea, and why this area is oil and gas rich. Coal-bearing rocks have been drawn down to depths of 5-10 kilometres and have been cooked, driving off precious fluid hydrocarbons that have conveniently become trapped in the shallower, porous sedimentary rocks such as in the Maui Field and Kupe Field. The sag also explains why the Marlborough Sounds are drowned and, in part, why we have Cook Strait.

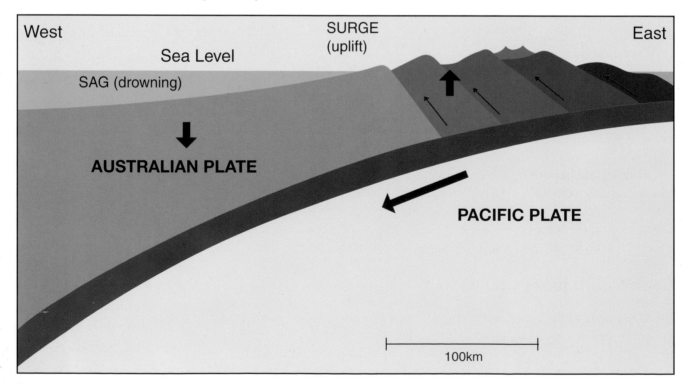

What would happen if subduction was suddenly switched off in New Zealand? Our volcanoes would cease to be active. Our mountain ranges would stop rising, slowly collapsing to form a more subdued landscape. Earthquake activity would diminish, and the big sag would pop back up to produce a lot more land, creating a single, much larger New Zealand landmass – perhaps a bit more like Australia!

## Cook Strait: just a mechanical interchange

What happens at the end of a subduction zone? More specifically, what happens at the southern termination of the subduction zone in New Zealand? The mechanism somehow changes, as a result of the changes in plate motion.

The transition zone between the crust-consuming oblique subduction zone in

*The Marlborough Sounds, looking south. This landscape is not 'drowned' due to a rise in sea level. It is part of a giant mechanical interchange within the plate boundary zone and it is also at the margin of a giant sag associated with subduction of the Pacific Plate beneath the Australian Plate. (IGNS)*

## Grinding the gears

The best way to think of changes in plate motion is to imagine that the Pacific Plate is a huge cogged wheel rotating anti-clockwise about an axle, and moving past another wheel, the Australian Plate, which is relatively fixed. Points (or vectors) on the Pacific wheel slowly change their angle of convergence as the wheel turns and moves towards the Australian wheel.

When the angle of convergence of the two wheels is more or less at right angles, subduction occurs. As this angle changes, more and more slippage occurs until ultimately the angle of wheel convergence is parallel and they actually slide past each other. Beyond this point, the wheels diverge and pull apart.

North of New Zealand there is head-to-head plate collision. In the North Island plate collision is at an oblique angle, which steadily increases until the plates are sliding past each other, as in much of the South Island.

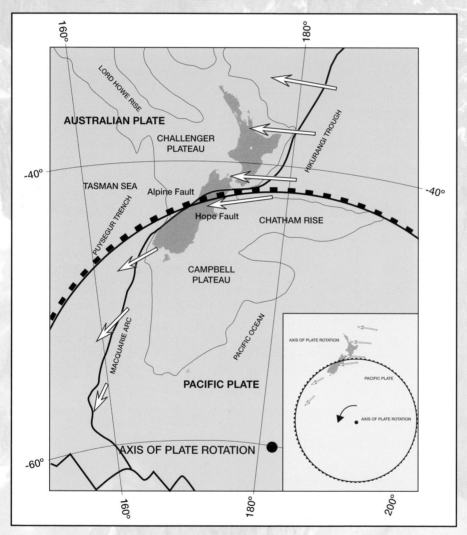

Geophysicists have established that the relative motion of the Pacific and Australian Plates in the New Zealand region can be described in terms of two huge cogs rotating towards each other about a common axis located to the southeast of New Zealand. This diagram illustrates the process and elegantly explains the various parts of the plate boundary zone in the New Zealand landscape. The North Island is dominated by subduction, the South Island by sliding on the Alpine Fault, and the Cook Strait region is a zone of mechanical interchange. The two plates are actually moving at different rates and in different directions with respect to each other but are nevertheless in collision. The Australian Plate is moving north and the Pacific Plate is moving west. What we see is a consequence of relative motion between them. (IGNS)

the southern North Island and the horizontal slippage along several massive fault zones in the northern South Island all comes together at Cook Strait. Most faults in New Zealand show movement in both vertical and horizontal directions. Plate motion is causing the crust to move up and sideways

simultaneously. Cook Strait is part of this process. It is a transition zone, where the forces associated with both subduction and horizontal sliding are too weak to push up and support mountains. This zone is probably gradually moving south as a natural consequence of changes in plate motion. Imagine some time in the future a Marlborough Sounds-like topography extending up the Wairau, Awatere, and Clarence Rivers!

The Marlborough Sounds are really mountain ranges. They show all the signs of a 'drowned' landscape, but they are not being flooded due to a rise in sea level. They are suffering from collapse of the crust, which drags the valleys down below sea level. They also happen to be at the southern end of the big sag, and therefore are doubly afflicted by processes that are trying to bring them down.

So Cook Strait is the product of a giant mechanical interchange. Further south the Alpine Fault takes over the role as the major horizontal slip zone along the plate boundary.

*The Hope Fault is responsible for the striking change in topography between the Seaward Kaikoura Mountains (left) and the gentle farmland inland of Kaikoura (right). This is the most active fault within the plate collision zone in the northern South Island. It proxies as the present boundary between the Australian and Pacific plates. (IGNS)*

# The Alpine Fault: the ultimate grinding edge

It is hard to imagine one landmass sliding past another. Our difficulty is trying to visualise it when we can't see it happening. The process is not smooth: it happens in fits and starts. Nor is it very fast: the rate at which it operates is barely perceptible – just tens of millimetres per year. Nevertheless, it happens, and there is ample geological evidence for it.

Geologist Harold Wellman was the first person to recognise the Alpine Fault as the surface expression of two major blocks of crust sliding past each other. He demonstrated that this sharply defined incision in the landscape can be traced from Marlborough to Fiordland, and that it dislocates the same distinctive belts of rock by at least 480 kilometres.

Viewed from space, the Alpine Fault stands out as a distinct line, one of the longest and straightest on the surface of the Earth. It is a livid knife-cut through the landscape, truncating everything in its path. It can be traced on land from the entrance to Milford Sound in the southern Tasman Sea, to Cloudy Bay on Cook Strait. The nearest big town to the Alpine Fault is Blenheim. The fault runs out into Cook Strait and is thought to connect indirectly with the Hikurangi Trough.

The Alpine Fault represents that section of the plate boundary along which the imaginary wheels are moving parallel to each other (see diagram on page 14). The latest rates of lateral slippage along the Alpine Fault have come from Global Positioning System (GPS) satellites. They show that Christchurch has moved south-west relative to Hokitika (the nearest biggest town on the other side of the Fault) by 46 millimetres in just 18 months! But relative to the South Pole, Hokitika is slowly heading north, towards the tropics. (Not so fast that the residents of Hokitika can start sipping pina coladas just yet, though! They'll have to wait another 600,000 years before they can grow pineapples.)

The plates are also pushing hard against each other, never more so than in the central part of the Southern Alps where our highest mountains are found: Mt Cook (3,754 metres) and Mt Tasman (3,497 metres). This is the zone of maximum collision and uplift. As with all mountain ranges, the Southern Alps are being pushed up and held up by tectonic forces. Erosion of these mountains through normal processes, including landslides and nasty weather, is happening at more or less the same rate as the uplift, and produces the spikiness of mountain ridges.

Inevitably as one travels south-west down the Alpine Fault, the effects of collision diminish. Off the shore of Fiordland there is another Cook Strait-like mechanical interchange, a zone in which the tectonic forces are insufficient to raise the crust above sea level.

## Living on the edge

New Zealand straddles the boundary zone between two gigantic crustal plates. It is a dynamic land, a wonderful natural laboratory where we can observe the effects of the titanic forces of the Earth at play. Our varied, particular, dramatic landscape is explained!

Subduction dominates the North Island, collision and lateral offset dominate the South Island, and the mechanical interchange between these two major effects largely explains the submergence of the Cook Strait region.

The natural hazards discussed in this book all relate to New Zealand's unique crustal make-up and position in relation to this boundary zone and the confrontation with weather rolling in from the west. The underlying big force at work is plate motion. It is a relentlessly moving process and it operates in tandem with gravity. These forces are not unique to New Zealand: they are truly global.

The more we know about these processes, the better we can determine how to live with them. We have been quick to exploit the effects of these processes, but understanding them is another matter. Still, we are getting better at predicting major earth hazards in New Zealand because our knowledge of the processes involved is improving all the time. The future is a much better-defined quantity than ever before, as are the hazards described in this book – not that this knowledge in any way diminishes their frightening reality when they do strike!

*The expression of the southern end of the Alpine Fault on land. Here it can be seen cutting across Lake McKerrow and heading out to sea north of the entrance to Milford Sound. This view is looking south-west into another transition zone of mechanical interchange within the plate boundary. As with Cook Strait, this is a transitional area, from sliding of the plates along the Alpine Fault to subduction. The tectonic forces are insufficient to push the crust up above the sea, hence the absence of land west of Fiordland.*

# Blow up!

BRUCE HOUGHTON AND DAVID JOHNSTON

During the night of 9-10 June 1886, people in the Rotorua area were woken by strong earthquakes. The ground seemed agitated, the air thick. Tourists who had come to the region to view the spectacular Pink and White Terraces, reputedly one of the great natural wonders of the world, became concerned by the extraordinary earth movements. Those from Britain and Europe had no knowledge of such things, since their homelands almost never receive the unpredictable jolting of ground tremors.

Before dawn light a huge black cloud lit by lightning and fireballs burst from the triple domes of Mt Tarawera. A massive eruption was under way, splitting the mountain open and spewing out shattered lava. Then Rotomahana, the lake into which the Terraces flowed, went skywards in a huge blast of steam and mud.

*The craters of Mount Tarawera and Lake Rotomahana as seen today, looking to the south.* (IGNS)

Opposite: *An explosive eruption column, Mount Ngauruhoe, 1974.* (IGNS)

The eruption lasted only six hours and by New Zealand standards was a relatively small one. But in this time a rift 17-kilometres long opened up, stretching from Waimangu to Mt Tarawera itself. You can see it today, as if some giant has taken a knife to a piece of landscape, slit it, and folded it open.

The drama of the scene continued to unfold. The surrounding landscape up to ten kilometres away was plastered with a layer of ash and mud a metre or more thick. The contents of Rotomahana and the valley in which it lay, including the Pink and White Terraces, were blasted out. A much larger Lake Rotomahana soon filled the crater left behind, flooding the whole valley. Two of New Zealand's largest hot springs can now be found at Waimangu in craters formed by the eruption.

Apart from these catastrophic impacts on the landscape, what had been witnessed was, in human terms, New Zealand's most lethal volcanic eruption.

*Top left: The people of Te Ariki village prior to the eruption of Mount Tarawera on 10 June 1886. Mount Tarawera can be seen in the background. (Burton Brothers Collection, Te Papa)*

*Top right: The White Terraces. Together with the Pink Terraces, these were a major tourist attraction in the nineteenth century. (Muir and Moodie Collection, Te Papa)*

*Bottom left and right: Te Wairoa Hotel before and after the Tarawera eruption. (Burton Brothers Collection, Te Papa)*

The tourist village of Te Wairoa and a host of small Māori settlements, including Te Ariki, were either wiped out or had suffered major destruction, buried beneath mud and ash. In the aftermath, 120 people were said to have been killed in the eruption (a figure based on body counts by European settlers). But Ngāti Hinemihi oral accounts put the death toll in the thousands, mostly in small villages that Pākehā never visited.

The awesome force of an exploding mountain had struck at the new colony's tourism heart.

## Volcanoes – shields, cones, caldera, and fields

We all know what they look like. The classic distinctive steep cone-shape of Ngauruhoe looming over the tussock of the central plateau of the North Island announces itself as being no ordinary hill. But what exactly are volcanoes?

The word itself is derived from the name of a Roman god, Vulcan, the god of fire. In simple terms, volcanoes are the surface manifestation of a direct or indirect connection to the hot interior of the Earth. The process of volcanism is one of transfer of magma, that is, molten rock, to the Earth's surface, and of its discharge. Volcanoes are the landform created as a by-product of this process.

Volcanologists use the word volcano to mean both the vent which is in eruption and the deposits that form around the vent. Most volcanoes are associated with the movement of large amounts of magma through the rigid crust of the Earth, either at the edges of the Earth's tectonic plates – for instance, Ruapehu, Tarawera, Taupo or, more rarely, in the interior of a plate, such as the young Auckland Volcanic Field, or the older extinct volcanoes of Banks Peninsula and Dunedin.

*The area affected by volcanic ash from the Tarawera Eruption.*
*(Te Papa)*

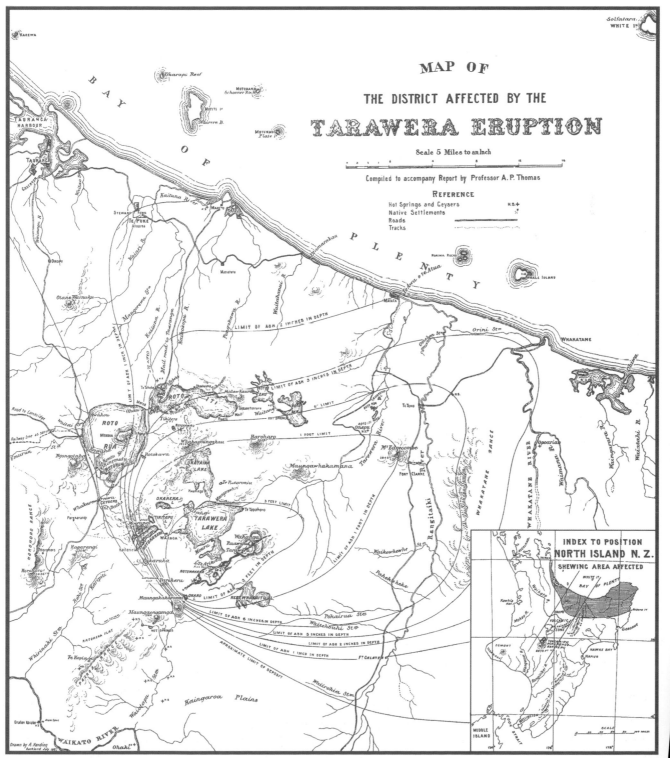

When the crustal plates of the Earth are torn apart, new molten magma rises up to heal the gash. This process forms large shield volcanoes, such as Iceland or the African Rift valley. These are places where new crust is being created, upwelling to the surface from the mantle. The mid-ocean ridges, those mostly submerged zipper-like lines of bubbling effusive volcanism, best categorise the notion of shield volcanoes. The East Pacific Rise and the mid-Atlantic Ridge are two good examples of where the very youngest of Earth's rocks are to be found. Heavy, frothy iron and magnesium-rich basaltic rocks well out and cool in the depths of the ocean, adding to the trailing edge of the plates.

Shield volcanoes have a broad and gentle profile, and are typically built from accumulations of numerous, thin lava flows. Shield volcanoes have few explosive eruptions and their numerous vents typically line up to form rift zones crossing

# Volcanoes in working order

**All New Zealand's active volcanoes are in the northern part of the country**

Whangarei volcanoes

Bay of Islands/Kaikohe volcanoes

Rumbles submarine volcanoes

Auckland volcanoes

Mayor Island

White Island

Haroharo

Edgecumbe

Tarawera

Taupo

Tongariro

Ngauruhoe

Ruapehu

Taranaki

Australian Plate

Pacific Plate

**Crater**
the blast area around the vent

**Vent**
the point of exit for magma at the surface

## Hot plumbing
re's the basic plumbing
a typical New Zealand
cone volcano.

**Cone**
the pile built, layer
upon layer, by the 'fall-
out' from eruptions

**Magma pipe**
the feed pipe for
magma to get to
the surface

**Magma chamber**
a storage tank for the magma
– usually some 7–10 kilometres
below Earth's surface

## Crust consumption

The heavy sinking edge of the Pacific plate dives below the lighter edge of the Australian plate.

The sinking plate gets hotter as it goes deeper.

As it melts, it creates some of the gassy brew that feeds our volcanic zone.

### Magma and lava

The nearer the magma gets to the surface, the less squeezed by pressure it becomes. It's like taking the lid off a fizzy drink bottle. The gas bubbles inside the magma expand and expand – and whoosh! One erupting volcano!

the summit of the shields. Kilauea volcano in Hawaii is the classic example of a growing shield volcano. New Zealand has four large extinct shield volcanoes: Lyttelton and Akaroa on Banks Peninsula, the Dunedin volcano, and Chatham Island.

In the few places on land where shield volcanoes are observed (Iceland and the African Rift valley), you can literally stand astride a crack in the Earth with one foot on one crustal plate, and the other on an adjacent one.

Some plates move more rapidly than others. If one plate contains less dense continental crust (rocks such as granite), the collision will drive the denser basaltic oceanic plate down into the mantle, in a process known as subduction. Deep below the surface these sinking basaltic rocks melt and create a series of new magma 'streamers' that find their way to the surface. The magma rises into the crust and then erupts at the surface to build cone and caldera volcanoes, typical volcanic types on the edges of subduction plates.

The word 'cone' is self-explanatory (think of an inverted ice-cream cone), and

*Volcanism is a function of tectonic processes deep within the Earth.*

(Awesome Forces exhibition, Te Papa)

# Eruptions from some of New Zealand's less active volcanoes

## Okataina Volcanic Centre

This volcanic centre has been active for over 400,000 years, and we have a good understanding of the last 21,000 years. Age is given in years before the present, from youngest to oldest.

| Age | Volume (in cubic kilometres) | Name of eruption |
|---|---|---|
| 112 | 1.5 | Tarawera Basalt (1886) |
| 700 | 3 | Kaharoa Tephra |
| 3500 | 0.5 | Rotokawa Basalt |
| 5500 | 13 | Whakatane Tephra |
| 7500 | 17 | Mamaku Tephra |
| 9000 | 8 | Rotoma Tephra |
| 11000 | 10 | Waiohau Tephra |
| 13500 | 4 | Rotorua Tephra |
| 15000 | 5 | Rerewhakaaitu Tephra |
| 18000 | 7 | Okareka Tephra |
| 21000 | 9 | Te Rere Tephra |

## Taupo Volcanic Centre

This volcanic centre has been active for over 300,000 years, and we have a good understanding of the last 26,500 years. Age is given in years before the present, from youngest to oldest.

| Age | Volume (in cubic kilometres) | Name of eruption |
|---|---|---|
| 1820 | 0.28 | |
| 1850 | 44.8 | Taupo 1800-year event (181 AD) |
| 2150 | 0.8 | Mapara Tephra |
| 2650 | 0.02 | |
| 2700 | 0.8 | Whakaipo Tephra |
| 2750 | 0.2 | |
| 3000 | 0.08 | |
| 3300 | 16.9 | Waimihia Tephra |
| 3950 | 0.05 | |
| 4050 | 0.15 | |
| 4100 | 0.05 | |
| 4150 | 0.05 | |
| 4200 | 0.15 | |
| 4500 | 0.2 | |
| 4550 | 0.07 | |
| 4600 | 0.35 | |
| 4620 | 0.015 | |
| 5200 | 0.02 | |
| 5300 | 0.2 | |
| 5800 | 0.5 | |
| 6150 | 0.12 | |
| 9050 | 4.8 | Opepe Tephra |
| 9780 | 0.2 | |
| 9800 | 0.75 | Poronui Tephra |
| 10100 | 1.4 | Karapiti Tephra |
| 14200 | 0.01 | |
| 15600 | 0.1 | |
| 17200 | 0.05 | |
| 26500 | >500 | Oruanui (Kawakawa Tephra) |

## Taranaki (Egmont) Volcano

The eruptive history over the last 28,000 years is well known. These are small eruptions, all with volumes of less than 1 cubic kilometre. Age is given in years before the present, from youngest to oldest.

| Age | Name of eruption |
|---|---|
| 3050 to 3100 | Manganui Tephra |
| c. 3600 | Inglewood Tephra |
| c. 4100 | Korito Tephra |
| 4400 | Mangatoki Tephra |
| c.4600-4700 | Tariki Tephra |
| c. 5200 | Waipuku Tephra |
| 8000 to 10000 | Kaponga Tephra |
| c. 10100 | Konini Tephra |
| c. 11000 | Mahoe Tephra |
| 12900 | Kaihouri Tephra |
| 19400 to 20200 | Paetahi Tephra |
| 20900 to 22700 | Poto Tephra |
| 23400 | Tuikonga Tephra |
| c. 24800-25200 | Koru Tephra |
| 26200 | Pukeiti Tephra |
| 27500-28000 | Waitepuku Tephra |

Some smaller eruptions are known, younger than 3,000 years, but have not been listed.

'caldera' is straightforward enough when you know it comes from a Spanish word meaning 'cauldron'. These subduction volcanoes are well represented in New Zealand. Ruapehu, Tongariro, Ngauruhoe, Taranaki (Egmont), Edgecumbe, and White Island are all cones, while Taupo and Okataina are classic calderas, or 'holes in the ground'. Unlike the basalts of the shield volcanoes, cones erupt

mostly andesitic lavas, while calderas produce mostly rhyolitic lavas with a much higher silica content than andesitic lavas.

Composite cone volcanoes such as Taranaki and Ruapehu have had a succession of small to moderate eruptions from a cluster of vents in roughly the same place. The lava and ash erupted by the vents build up close by to form a large cone, which is the volcano itself. The magma takes roughly the same route to reach the surface in each eruption, so the site of future eruptions can usually be predicted. Over a longer period of time several cones may form, overlapping and building on top of one other. Mt Ngauruhoe, for instance, is really just a new cone on the flanks of the more massive Tongariro.

Caldera volcanoes such as Okataina (which includes Mt Tarawera) or Taupo have a history of moderate to large eruptions. Eruptions from these volcanoes are

*Mt Taranaki (Egmont) is the second-largest cone volcano in New Zealand and at 2,518 metres is the second-highest mountain in the North Island. The upper flanks of Mt Taranaki consist of alternating layers of lava and loose volcanic ash which have built up into the cone we see today. Mt Taranaki is considered dormant, since the latest eruption in which magma reached the surface is thought to have occurred in 1755 AD, just before the arrival of Europeans in this country. The parasitic cone Fanthams Peak can be seen in the foreground.*
(IGNS)

*Mt Tarawera, a cluster of rhyolitic domes. It was most recently active in 1886, and before that 650 years ago.*
(IGNS)

occasionally so large that the ground surface collapses into a hole (the caldera). The hole replaces the underground reservoir that the magma came out of. In the case of Taupo, the caldera is now filled by the lake. The material that comes out is usually spread so far and wide that no large cone forms, but lavas may pile up on top of each other inside the caldera to form domes. Mt Tarawera is a good example of a dome volcano. In large, caldera-forming eruptions, a lot of the erupted material accumulates within the caldera itself as it collapses, so that the old land surface may be buried to a depth of more than one kilometre. Domes often form steep-sided islands in caldera lakes, for example Motutaiko Island in Taupo.

Volcanic fields (such as the one that Auckland city sits on) are places where small basaltic eruptions occur over a wide geographic area, and are spaced over long time intervals (many thousands of years). These 'hot spot' volcanoes are surface expressions of a fixed connection to the mantle. In other words, magma rises upwards from the same place in the mantle. Any variation in the distribution of surface volcanoes reflects slightly altered pathways up cracks to the surface, or movement of the surface by tectonic action. Each eruption builds a single small volcano (such as Mount Eden, One Tree Hill, or Rangitoto) which does not erupt again. The next eruption in the field occurs in a different place, and the site cannot be predicted until the eruption is imminent.

## Time and size

Probably the key evidence observed by geologists and the most striking feature of this volcano-creating process is the 'Ring of Fire' which marks the descent of the Pacific Plate beneath its neighbours, forming chains of volcanoes in Chile, Alaska, the Philippines, Japan, Indonesia, and the central North Island of New Zealand.

The volcanoes in New Zealand are not randomly scattered, but are grouped into areas of intense activity that relate to the movement of the large crustal plates in the Southwest Pacific. Most young volcanoes on land lie between White Island and Ruapehu in the Taupo Volcanic Zone

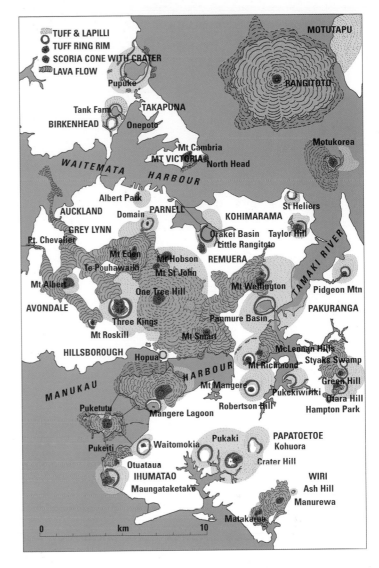

*A map of the Auckland Volcanic Field.*
*(IGNS)*

*A horseshoe crater, one of two on One Tree Hill. These craters were not breached by an outburst of lava, but grew in a horseshoe shape as vigorous out-flowings of lava prevented erupted material from accumulating by carrying it away. The symmetrical lava cone of Rangitoto is visible in the background.*
*(IGNS)*

(TVZ), and are aligned parallel to the edge of the Pacific Plate. Others, like Auckland and Northland, are 'intra-plate' volcanoes, in the middle of a plate. On the sea-floor off the Bay of Plenty coast there are many more volcanic cones. These submarine volcanoes are the offshore extension of the TVZ, which stretches all the way to the Equator.

New Zealand's young volcanoes represent a cross-section of most of the types of volcanoes documented elsewhere in the world. In fact, the only one we don't have is an example of an active shield volcano, such as Kilauea or Mauna Loa in Hawaii. In two respects, New Zealand's volcanoes are world-beaters. Our cone volcanoes at Ruapehu, Ngauruhoe and White Island are among the most frequently active volcanoes known; while Taupo and Okataina are the most productive caldera volcanoes on Earth. This high frequency and productivity of eruptions in the central North Island is a function of the fact that the Earth's crust is very thin (only 15-20 kilometres thick, versus 35-45 kilometres thick for a normal continent) and it is being rapidly torn apart by plate tectonic processes.

*Mt Eden (Maungawhau), the highest point (196 metres high) in Auckland City, is a large scoria cone with a well-formed summit crater. Its slopes were terraced by Māori, who found them easy to excavate. Food storage pits can be seen on the foreground slope. Auckland's highly vulnerable commercial and business centre is visible behind Mt Eden bordering the Waitemata Harbour, with the North Shore beyond. (IGNS)*

*Browns Island (Motukorea) in the Inner Hauraki Gulf, close to Auckland City, is a scoria cone with a well-formed main crater. A tuff ring remnant can be seen as a prominent ridge to the left of the cone, and there is a small lava field to the right. Auckland's eastern suburbs are visible on the far right of the picture. (IGNS)*

White Island, New Zealand's most active cone volcano, has been in a state of frequent eruption since December 1976. The eruptions are mostly small, which means the hazard zones are restricted to the island itself, but dustings of volcanic ash occasionally fall on the mainland. The white clouds are highly acidic gases given off by the volcano. (IGNS)

Not all volcanic eruptions are created equal. One of the exciting things about volcanism is the vast range of scales on which it operates. While in everyday life we think in terms of simple multiplications (such as 'twice my salary' or 'three times as many cars on the road'), in volcanology we use orders of magnitude. Ten times is one order of magnitude, 100 times is two orders of magnitude, 1000 times is three, and so on. The size, intensity, and duration of eruptions vary enormously, by seven or eight orders of magnitude.

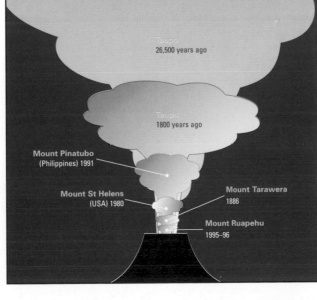

## Ash cloud cover

By measuring the depth of ash layers on land and sea, scientists work out how much volcanic material has been blasted into the atmosphere during volcanic eruptions.

Compare the sizes of volcanic ash clouds made by Taupo eruptions with some other recent eruptions.

Taupo
26,500 years ago

Taupo
1800 years ago

Mount Pinatubo
(Philippines) 1991

Mount St Helens
(USA) 1980

Mount Tarawera
1886

Mount Ruapehu
1995–96

How big is big? The plumes show the relative size of some well-known eruptions compared with the great volumes ejected by the Taupo caldera.

(Te Papa)

The largest eruptions known have ejected 2,000 cubic kilometres of molten rock (such as the huge Whakamaru Eruption from north of Taupo, 350,000 years ago), whereas the smallest ones spat out a mere 1,000 cubic metres of rock (such as the many small explosions from Ruapehu in the 1970s and 1980s). That makes the largest known eruption some 1,000,000,000 times bigger than the smallest!

Some eruptions have gone on nearly continuously for more than five years, while others last less than five seconds (such as some small explosions from Ruapehu). Many eruptions last only a few days, but White Island has been continuously active for several years at a time (most recently from 1986 to 1992), in a mild kind of way.

*A lava eruption, Mount Ngauruhoe, 1954.*
(IGNS)

## How do volcanoes erupt?

Unlike other natural hazards like earthquakes or landslides that may be all over in minutes, volcanic eruptions last a relatively long time (for days, months, or even years) and affect a large area (hundreds or thousands of square kilometres). Fortunately they also come with their own warning signs, such as ground deformation, earthquakes, and temperature changes.

Understanding eruptions comes down to understanding the characteristics of one natural substance: magma. Magma is molten rock – a complex, dynamic mixture of components. Magma consists of the liquid itself, the gas dissolved in it, and the solid particles (crystals and rock fragments) suspended in it.

There are two main kinds of volcanic eruption: effusive and explosive. In an effusive eruption, liquid magma oozes from the Earth's surface to form a lava flow. If there's very little gas in the magma, or if it is so fluid that gases can easily escape, a lava flow is the likely end product. In contrast, an explosive eruption is violent. Expanding gases tear the magma apart, and a stream of gas and rock fragments erupts. The fragments are called pyroclasts (from the Greek words for 'fiery' and 'broken').

Volcanic explosions are caused by two mechanisms. The first involves the rapid release of the volcanic gases originally dissolved in the magma and held trapped by the pressure of the rock around it. The pressure decreases as the magma rises to the surface, and tiny gas bubbles form. These bubbles expand, merge together, and grow until the magma is essentially a foam. If the bubbles expand still further, the froth is ripped apart into a mixture of hot gas and liquid droplets. We call these 'magmatic explosions'. They involve gas that is internal to the magma, that is, the gas comes from within the melt itself.

The second mechanism causing a volcanic explosion involves an external source for the exploding gas – water that can be flashed into steam. The water is either surface water in lakes or streams, or the groundwater held in pores and cracks within the shallow rocks. On the Earth's surface, water is a liquid. But if it is heated to 1,000°C when it comes into contact with magma, and then released to atmospheric pressure, it becomes a vapour occupying a volume 10,000 times larger. So add water to hot magma and you have a recipe for disaster!

## A hazardous place

An individual eruption typically creates several quite different kinds of hazard, each of which poses a different threat to the community.

### Lava

If the magma doesn't contain much gas by the time it reaches the surface, it is discharged quietly as a fluid, hot toothpaste-like flow, rather than explosively. Lava flows run down valleys, but relatively slowly – it's often possible for a person to out-run a moving lava flow.

*An effusive, viscous lava flow, typical of basalt volcanoes. This one is from Kilauea volcano in Hawaii.*
*(USGS)*

### Pyroclastic fall

Volcanic ash is carried far and wide in a powerful jet of hot, rapidly expanding gas. The ash is light and, depending on the wind's strength and direction, it can cover an area as big as 100,000 square kilometres. The particles are carried to great heights by the expanding and cooling gas, from a few kilometres high to a few tens of kilometres, and they settle slowly. An erupting vent will be surrounded by a wide zone in which ash and pumice may fall, though the location and shape of the zone is strongly influenced by how strong the wind is and which direction it is blowing in. Only a few millimetres or centimetres of ash falling on towns and cities is enough to disrupt transport, electricity, water, sewage, and stormwater systems. Volcanic ash is highly abrasive, mildly corrosive, and potentially conductive (especially when it is wet). However, if the ash fall is thin (less than 50 millimetres thick), most facilities can be restored within a few days or weeks after an eruption has ended.

### Pyroclastic density currents

Many violent eruptions are accompanied by ground-hugging flows of hot rock fragments and gas. Their deposits are known as ignimbrites, and they form billowing

clouds moving across the ground like hot avalanches. The temperature can vary from 100°C to more than 700°C. You couldn't hope to out-run flows like this. They can reach speeds of 50 to 150 kilometres per hour and are probably the most frightening and lethal events associated with large eruptions.

## Hydrothermal explosions

What happens in a hydrothermal eruption resembles what happens when you take the lid off a pressure-cooker. A large geothermal system may contain several cubic kilometres of water, below ground and under pressure. If the pressure increases, because of an earthquake or magma welling up, the rapid release of pressure can blow the lid off. However, compared with the explosive force of a rhyolitic eruption, hydrothermal eruptions are weak. Only small quantities of material are ejected, reaching a few hundred metres from the source.

## Sector collapses

Volcanoes can form rapidly, and steep volcanic cones and domes are often unstable landforms. If a portion of the volcano collapses suddenly, the result can be catastrophic, generating large rock slides from the volcano called debris avalanches. The collapse may have been triggered by the intrusion of magma, the shaking from an earthquake, gradual weakening due to hydrothermal alteration, or even heavy rain which may saturate and weaken parts of the cone.

*Eruption column, Mount Ngauruhoe, 1974. (IGNS)*

*Mt Ngauruhoe is a young cone volcano (less than 2,500 years old) that has been built up by numerous eruptions of lava, volcanic ash, and pyroclastic density currents. The ash and gas billowing down the flanks of Mt Ngauruhoe are a ground-hugging pyroclastic density current, which was generated during its most recent eruption in 1975. (IGNS)*

## Lahars and floods

In human and economic terms, some of the worst disasters caused by volcanoes are the result of lahars, mud flows and floods that occur during and after large eruptions. Lahars are rapidly moving slurries of ice, water, mud, and extraneous rocks and boulders picked up in the force of the flow. Generally they are short-lived, being an initial response to the violent outpouring of an eruption. Their destructive capability is legendary.

On Christmas Eve 1953, a portion of the ice, rock, and debris wall of Ruapehu's Crater Lake, formed after the 1945 eruption, suddenly collapsed, but not as a result of an explosion. Some 340,000 cubic metres of water was released through an ice cave and rushed down the Whangaehu River. Travelling down an ancient well-established lahar route, the flow had little impact on the surrounding countryside, until at 10.20 pm it cascaded into the Tangiwai rail bridge, knocking out a number of structural supports. The weight of the scheduled Wellington-Auckland express train collapsed the bridge, culminating in New Zealand's worst rail disaster, with the loss of 151 lives. One of the carriages was transported 2.4 kilometres downstream and a 125-tonne bridge pile was shifted 64 metres sideways. Lahars are lethal rivers of destruction just waiting to happen.

Floods are a frequent consequence of crater breaching, with periodic flash floods that can go on for a period of years or even decades. Recent examples are the floods from Mt Pinatubo in the Philippines that have happened regularly since the eruption in 1991. These have had an enormous human and financial cost.

Cone volcanoes like Ruapehu and Taranaki produce a lot of sediment. They attract high rainfall, and are drained by rapid, energetic streams that readily redistribute volcanic debris over the surrounding area. But Taupo caldera takes the prize for flooding – after the Taupo eruption 1800 years ago, there were major episodes of flooding and sedimentation in all the large rivers of the North Island.

*A spectacular hydrothermal eruption occurring in 1904 at Waimangu Geyser, near Lake Rotomahana.*
*(Beattie and Co. Collection, Te Papa)*

### Volcanic gas

Volcanic gases consist mostly of steam, plus some carbon dioxide and various compounds of chlorine and sulphur. Small amounts of carbon monoxide, fluorine, and other compounds are also released. Some of these gases are poisonous or corrosive, and are dangerous to living things. Many gases are trapped with the falling ash as acidic water droplets.

## Some of the biggest blow-ups known!

Taupo volcano is the most frequently active and productive rhyolite volcano in the world. It is a caldera-type volcano occupying about the same area as metropolitan Auckland.

Taupo first began erupting about 300,000 years ago, following a series of huge explosions from an area north of present day Lake Taupo. These produced the ignimbrite deposits seen in the impressive cliffs around the western side of the lake. This highly siliceous rhyolitic rock forms when the unstable eruption column ceases to rise higher into the air and collapses back to earth. As it does so it rushes out and away from the vent as a pyroclastic density current, depositing as consolidated ignimbrite.

Between 120,000 and 65,000 years ago, volcanic activity started to increase, with pyroclastic flows and lava domes progressively building the surrounding landscape. These more explosive eruptions climaxed 26,500 years ago in the huge Oruanui or Kawakawa Eruption.

## Taupo – the Oruanui Eruption

The Oruanui is the biggest eruption known from Taupo. It produced a huge fall deposit and a large ignimbrite (pyroclastic density current) deposit that buried much of the central North Island to depths of up to 200 metres! The size of the eruption is difficult to grasp, but roughly 800 cubic kilometres of pumice and ash were ejected in this one event, probably over a period of a few days or weeks. That's enough to construct three Ruapehu-sized cones! So extensive was the deposit of fall material that seafloor samples taken in nearly 4,300 metres of water south of the Chatham Islands, over 1,000 kilometres away from the eruption centre, reveal a coloured layer of Oruanui ash up to 6 centimetres thick. The ash would have been blown by the wind to the Chathams and then dispersed by ocean currents, so a layer of ash this thick that is identifiable at such a depth testifies to the enormous scale of the event.

The rapid eruption of so much material caused several hundred square kilometres of the area around the vent to collapse to form the Lake Taupo basin, which is now partly infilled by the lake. The old land surface is now buried many hundreds of metres below the floor of Lake Taupo.

There were another 26 smaller eruptions after the Oruanui and before the next cataclysmic blast, the Taupo 1,800-year event.

*Opposite: A gas vent on White Island.* (IGNS)

## Taupo – the eruption 1800 years ago

This eruption was centred on vents near the Horomatangi Reefs, now submerged beneath Lake Taupo. It is the second largest eruption from the volcano and the most violent eruption anywhere in the world in the last 5,000 years. At times, the eruption column reached high into the stratosphere, over 50 kilometres – nearly twice as high as the well documented eruption column of Mt St Helens in Washington, USA – and the highest eruption column theoretically possible. The eruption culminated in a catastrophic pyroclastic density current of hot ash and pumice that devastated 20,000 square kilometres of the central North Island, including rain forest that had been undisturbed since the last Ice Age, 10,000 years ago.

Floods associated with the eruption barrelled down all the major rivers of the North Island and the sites of the present-day cities of Napier, Hastings, and Wanganui were buried under a layer of volcanic silt. Were this same eruption to occur today, with the same westerly wind directions, fall deposits would cause chaos to an area from Hamilton to Palmerston North, now populated by over 200,000 people. From Rotorua to Gisborne buildings would be damaged or destroyed and farmlands would be smothered.

The high speed of the pyroclastic density current gave it a momentum that carried it with ease over mountains more than 1,500 metres high. Mt Ruapehu was the only mountain nearby high enough to block or divert the flow.

*A layer cake of pumice deposits, as seen in road cuttings to the east of Taupo, showing a succession of at least six separate eruptions. (Awesome Forces exhibition, Te Papa)*

*The extent of the Oruanui Eruption of 26,500 years ago, the largest recognised Taupo eruption. (IGNS)*

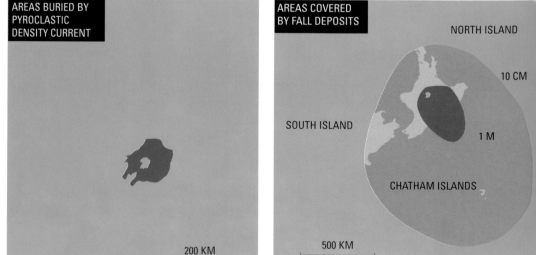

AREAS BURIED BY PYROCLASTIC DENSITY CURRENT

200 KM

AREAS COVERED BY FALL DEPOSITS

NORTH ISLAND

10 CM

SOUTH ISLAND

1 M

CHATHAM ISLANDS

500 KM

# Taupo – a blow by blow account

The Taupo 1,800-year ago event was a complex eruption that went through six distinct phases.

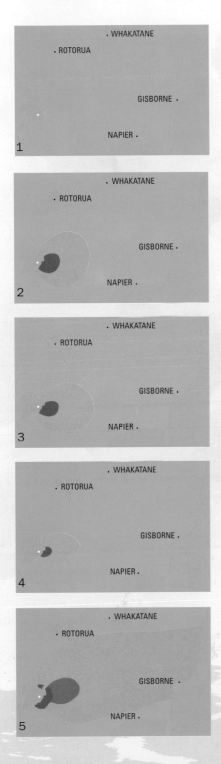

Stages of the Taupo Eruption. (IGNS)

**Phase 1:** The eruption began beneath the ancestral Lake Taupo, with minor explosions. Lake water mixed with a gas-rich foam of magma and generated a small fall deposit close to the lake. Fall deposits result when fragments of magma and old rocks surrounding the vent are carried up into an eruption plume. The plume may be blown sideways by the wind and the fragments fall to the ground. These blanket the landscape like a snowfall.

**Phase 2:** Magma pressure raised the vent above the lake, the rate of the eruption increased dramatically, and a high eruption column rained pumice over a wide area predominantly east (downwind) of the vent.

**Phase 3:** Lake water entering the vent mixed with the gas-charged magma foam, generating a thin white ash-rich pumice deposit. This stage was abruptly terminated, probably by water flooding deep into the vent.

**Phase 4:** Activity recommenced after a break of some hours to weeks when gas-poor magma met with lake water to produce a high, water-rich eruption plume.

**Phase 5:** The vent was again cleared of water as the eruption gathered intensity. A gigantic eruption column (50 kilometres high) rained pumice over an area extending from East Cape to Hawkes Bay. Parts of the column became unstable and collapsed to produce small pyroclastic density currents – ground-hugging, rapidly moving mixtures of ash, pumice, and hot gases sweeping outwards from the vent.

*The extent of the Taupo ignimbrite*

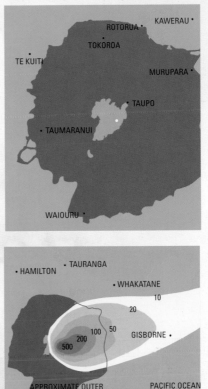

**Phase 6:** A further abrupt change produced a fountaining eruption plume and an extensive pyroclastic density current forming what is today known as the Taupo ignimbrite, the most violent pyroclastic density current yet recognised. This flow moved rapidly outwards from the vent at speeds of 600-900 kilometres per hour, and travelled 70-90 kilometres from the vent! Over 100,000,000 tonnes of pumice was released per second! Areas overrun by the flow were buried under hot pumice and ash; almost all vegetation was destroyed, and fragments of the former surrounding forest cover can be seen today as charred or carbonised logs in the ignimbrite. Most of the pumice we see around our coastline today came from this last phase of the eruption.

*Mount Ruapehu explodes into life on 23 September 1995, the first day that members of the public became aware that an eruption was under way. This spectacular photograph was taken by a skier. (Arthur Pengelly)*

The ignimbrite was deposited over the highest peaks of the Kaimanawa Range as well as over the top of Mt Tongariro, and ponded in valley bottoms. So powerful was this last stage of the eruption that it eroded deposits from earlier phases of the eruption.

The front of the Taupo flow would have looked like a huge turbulent wave, jetting forward at frightening speed. Some of the great film footage of the lethal Mt St Helens Eruption captures the enormous power of a pyroclastic flow, instilling fear into the hearts of any creature close enough to experience one of Earth's most impressive awesome forces.

## Ruapehu then and now

The 1945 and 1995-1996 Ruapehu Eruptions were the two largest volcanic events in New Zealand this century. The 1945 eruption was about the same size as the 1995-6 eruptions, but its effect was much less severe.

Both eruptions distributed ash over much of the North Island. The frequency of ash falls in many communities was greater in 1945 than in the 1995 and 1996 eruptions combined. However, the consequences were significantly greater in many places in 1995 and 1996. Individual ash falls were a few millimetres thick closest to the volcano (within a radius of 50 kilometres) and there were

only trace amounts falling further away. Despite their spectacular appearance, captured on nation-wide television, the 1995 and 1996 eruptions really were tiddlers. If you compare the millimetres left amongst vegetation on the Desert Road with the much thicker deposits from earlier explosions from Taupo, Ngauruhoe, Tongariro, and Ruapehu below this, it re-emphasises the huge scale of earlier events in this area.

Ash falls caused minor eye and throat irritations, soiled the interiors of houses, damaged the paintwork on houses and cars, damaged crops, and caused numerous disruptions to water and electricity supplies, air travel, and other forms of transport.

*Ash-laden river water spills into Lake Taupo near Turangi in 1995. (IGNS)*

New Zealand's population has doubled since 1945. Improvements in transportation and the development of recreational facilities have led to a massive increase in the number of people using Tongariro National Park. Three ski-fields now operate on the mountain, with more than 450,000 skier days per year. Back in 1945 there was only one field with a few thousand skier days per year. There were no ski lifts on the mountain in 1945, but by 1995 there were 36. The 1995 and 1996 eruptions resulted in the closure of all three fields. It was the ski-field closure that causing most of the losses to the regional economy – a deficit of more than $100 million.

The Tongariro power scheme, built between 1973 and 1983, uses a complex system of canals, tunnels, and lakes to collect water

*Even ash clouds have a silver lining! Kids bag up fresh Ruapehu ash samples for sale as eruption souvenirs.*

*(Evening Post)*

from the east, west, and south catchments on the flanks of Ruapehu, diverting it northwards for hydroelectric power generation. Damage to the electricity sector resulted in the second largest economic impact (about $20 million).

The use of air transport in New Zealand has undergone rapid growth in the past 50 years. In 1945, about 61,000 passengers travelled on scheduled flights each year. By 1995 the annual figure had risen to over 4.5 million passengers. Aircraft are extremely vulnerable to ash, particularly their jet engines, so the Civil Aviation Authority imposed an air-space restriction around Ruapehu in 1995 and 1996, disrupting the short-term plans of many thousands of travellers.

In 1945 the Desert Road, like most provincial roads, was unsealed, and vehicles travelled more slowly. Road transport has grown significantly, and fifty years later there were eight times the number of vehicles on this road. In 1945 the roads at the base of Ruapehu stayed open; in 1995 falling ash caused State Highway 1 to be closed three times.

Attitudes to public safety have changed in the last fifty years. At no time in 1945 were any access restrictions to the crater area imposed, despite the significant risk. (People were hit by flying blocks on at least two occasions.) These days the Department of Conservation has a responsibility for the safety of visitors to the National Park, and it responded accordingly, imposing a two-kilometre restriction around the crater during the 1995-6 eruptions. The New Zealand Geological Survey had only two geological staff permanently based at the volcano during the peak of activity in August 1945, compared with more than 30 IGNS personnel on duty there during the initial stages of the 1995 eruption.

*Gisborne schoolgirls muffle themselves against ash inhalation.*
(Gisborne Herald)

*Cleaning up the mess. Soldiers hose down buildings in Wairoa to remove the ash.*
(Wairoa Star)

## Warning, warning!

New Zealand contains a large number of active and potentially active volcanoes. The Ruapehu Eruptions in 1995 and 1996 have shown us first-hand the devastating effect of volcanic activity on the surrounding landscape and the people living there. Although we cannot accurately predict when the next eruption of any volcano may occur, we can assess its likely effects, and plan for them.

In New Zealand we are highly vulnerable to volcanic eruptions. Volcanologists refer to a 'volcanic crisis' as the whole sequence of events from the awakening of a volcano, the building up to an eruption, the eruption itself, through to its aftermath, as the affected region recovers. Still, crises are rare. Most volcanoes have long quiet intervals between eruptions, which may last from several years to many centuries. That means that most volcanoes are quiescent most of the time, and these quiet times are the best time to prepare people for what happens in an eruption.

Volcanic eruptions often show clear warning signals or precursors, but the

exact form a volcanic eruption will take is impossible to predict. Often two successive eruptions from a single volcano will be quite different in size and style, and will pose quite different levels of risk to the community. For instance, Mt Tarawera, usually a rhyolitic volcano, actually erupted basalt during the 1886 event. The origin of the magma was deeper into the mantle than the shallower material that typically forms andesitic and rhyolitic cones.

Opposite: *The 1996 Ruapehu eruption as seen from space.* (Landcare Research)

There is no easy way of estimating the size of a future event from the magnitude of the warning signs, either, and there are no rules for guessing how much time will elapse from the first precursor to the dangerous climax of an eruption. Given these uncertainties, then, how can we make the best use of the clear precursor warnings of a future volcanic eruption?

During a volcanic crisis, the demand for information is intense. Volcanic eruptions are spectacular events which are highly newsworthy, and it is vital that the media message accompanying eruption images conveys the true level of risk. When the available information is full of uncertainty (a common situation prior to an eruption and during an eruption) New Zealand's volcanologists avoid making unrealistic forecasts. Rumour control is critical.

The effects of eruptions can continue for decades. In particular, flooding and lahars may continue to affect areas for years following an eruption, as ash and rock is washed off the volcano. Individual property owners are covered by the Earthquake Commission (EQC) and are insured against loss or damage to their homes, up to a set limit, if they have an ordinary fire insurance policy. Organisations are responsible for dealing with the effects of an eruption on their property, however.

Some people around the world are affected by volcanic eruptions every day of their lives. Others, like most New Zealanders, only experience eruptions once or twice during their lifetime. In both cases there is a need to learn to co-exist with volcanoes and minimise the problems that they cause. The best solution is public education in the quiet periods between eruptions through television programmes, newspaper articles, and particularly projects like the Awesome Forces exhibition at Te Papa, which bring volcanoes and other natural hazards into focus, and (safely) into people's lives.

## Alert!

Volcano surveillance in the New Zealand region is carried out by the Institute of Geological and Nuclear Sciences (IGNS). Each volcano is assigned a Scientific Alert Level by IGNS, denoting the current status of the volcano. This is a 6-stage classification, where the lowest level is 0 (dormancy) and the highest level is 5 (large-scale hazardous eruption in progress). The New Zealand system has two parallel tables, one for frequently active cone volcanoes and the other for reawakening volcanoes. IGNS adjusts the alert level based on observations from key agencies and the surveillance programmes at each volcano and notifies Ministry of Civil Defence, local councils, and the media.

A change from Alert Level 0 to Alert Level 1 at any volcano does not necessarily mean that volcanic activity is imminent. Volcanoes can undergo long periods of unrest without eruptions. Pre-eruption crises in New Zealand and overseas have lasted from as little as two months to more than twenty years.

# The big one!

ALAN HULL

We interrupt this broadcast to bring you reports of a major earthquake that struck the capital a short time ago...

A sudden interruption like this to our daily lives is often the first indication that a large earthquake has happened. A brief announcement signals that the lives of thousands of people may have suddenly changed. Their relatives and loved ones may be missing, trapped or lying dead in a partially collapsed building; their homes may be damaged; while all the services needed to sustain normal daily life, such as power, water, gas, and telephone, may no longer function. All that was familiar and safe has changed dramatically in less than a few minutes.

A news item like this could come from any one of the major cities in the Asia Pacific region. Over the last hundred years news such as this has come from San Francisco and Los Angeles in the USA, Tokyo and Kobe in Japan, the Philippines, Chile, and several cities in eastern China, to mention just a few. In New Zealand the news of serious earthquake damage came from Napier in 1931, Inangahua in 1968, and Edgecumbe in 1987. Every resident of Wellington knows that one day the world will learn of the large earthquake that has hit their home town.

*A serious set of pot holes! Road damage sustained in the Hawke's Bay Earthquake of 1931.*
(Te Papa)

Opposite: *Surveying the damage wrought by an earthquake: treasured belongings smashed.*
(Ross Land, courtesy of Fotopacific)

## What are earthquakes?

Imagine that you are sitting in a boat near the edge of a small pond when a large rock is suddenly dropped into the middle of the pond. As the rock enters the water, waves or ripples of water radiate away from it, and after a short time the first of these waves starts to rock your boat. As each wave passes, the boat rises and falls. Eventually it stops moving when the rock has sunk to the bottom and there are no more waves being generated.

The shaking of an earthquake is the Earth vibrating as waves radiate away from a place where energy has been released suddenly. Sudden slippage along cracks or faults releases energy stored up by the slow straining of the rocks on either side of the crack. The release of energy causes the vibrations that we describe as an earthquake when we feel them on the Earth's surface.

# Why do earthquakes happen?

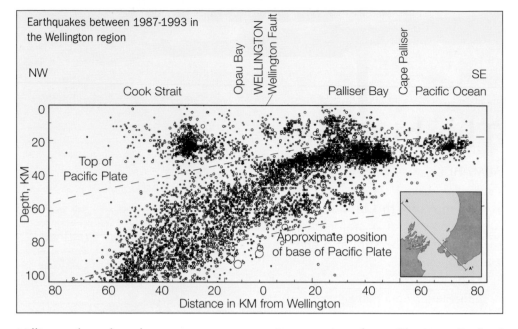

Millions of earthquakes occur every year. Some active places like New Zealand experience many more earthquakes than less active places like Australia and Antarctica. Why some places are more prone to earthquakes than others was a mystery until the development of the theory of Plate Tectonics in the late 1960s. According to Plate Tectonics, the surface of the Earth is made up of 15 large, rigid plates of rock anywhere from 15 to 100 kilometres thick. These plates are constantly moving with respect to each other, but slowly, at about 20-120 millimetres per year. At their edges the plates are continually bumping and grinding into each other, and the constant jostling causes stresses to accumulate in the brittle, upper layers of the plates. When the brittle rock finally breaks it generates earthquakes.

New Zealand sits astride the boundary of two of these great plates: the Pacific Plate to the east and the Australian Plate to the west. The zone of interaction of these plates is about 500

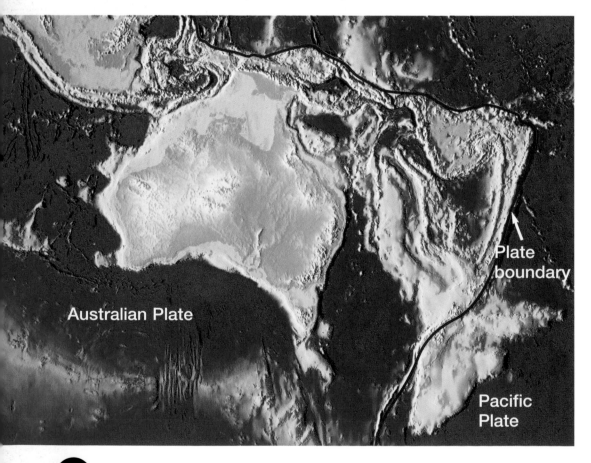

kilometres wide, and earthquakes can occur anywhere in this zone, at any time. The central part of New Zealand, with its high mountains and rugged hills, sits right on top of the main zone of plate interaction, so it experiences the most earthquakes, and the biggest ones. The plate interaction zone has many different cracks and ripples, and each one is potentially the source of moderate to large earthquakes.

## So what exactly is going on?

There are two main kinds of waves generated by an earthquake. The first are P (primary or push) waves, followed by S (secondary or shake) waves. P waves travel fast (about 20,000 kilometres per hour) from the earthquake source. Sound waves in air are P waves. Just like sound waves, earthquake P waves move by alternately compressing and expanding the particles of rock in the direction in which they are travelling. Indeed, when earthquake P waves reach the Earth's surface they often generate sound waves by compressing the particles of air as they emerge from the rock. People say they heard the earthquake coming, because they heard, rather than felt, the P wave. P waves do not generally cause much damage, except in the largest of earthquakes.

S waves travel at about half the speed of P waves, around 10,000 kilometres per hour, and are transmitted as a shearing motion at right angles to the direction of travel. To visualise the S waves, imagine you've tied a heavy rope to a post, and you're wiggling it from side to side. S waves cause damage when their side-to-side motion sways buildings and their contents.

Earthquake damage is caused by waves travelling near the surface of the Earth. Many people have reported seeing them travel along the ground in front of them, causing rumpling and undulation of the ground by as much as a metre as they pass. The horizontal motions of S waves are particularly damaging to buildings, as much of the building's weight is shifted sideways as the waves pass. Earthquake movements generated in the buildings can exceed the ability of the

A typical seismogram showing the fast P waves arriving first, followed by the slower S waves. These traces were all recorded in Wellington from the same earthquake, and they show the motion in the vertical, north/south, and east/west directions (from top to bottom). (IGNS)

columns to resist the sideways movement. When this happens a building may partially or completely collapse.

The difference in the travel speed of P and S waves explains the complex motions that people feel in an earthquake. When the earthquake is located some distance from you, the first wave to arrive is the P wave. This is the marked jolt that signals the onset of an earthquake, catches you by surprise and tells you instantly that if a big earthquake is occurring, there is much more to come. The next wave to arrive is the S wave. While you usually can't distinguish it from the surface waves following rapidly behind, it marks the onset of the strong shaking. Seismologists use this difference in travel time between P and S waves to estimate the distance between the earthquake source and the earthquake recording instrument.

In the biggest earthquakes, the seismic waves (P and S) can travel right through the Earth. As the seismic waves change from one internal Earth layer to another they bend, just like light does when travelling from water into air. Some waves from the biggest of earthquakes can bounce around inside the Earth for almost a month, making the Earth ring like a very large bell. However, you need special instruments to 'hear' the ring, because the tone is *very* low, at about 1 cycle per hour. (Compare this with the 256 cycles per second of middle C on a piano!)

## Earthquake scars in the landscape

Take a closer look at the rocks exposed along a walking path or along the rocky platform at the beach, and you'll see that in many places the rocks have fractures preserved within them. Some of these fractures record the cracking of the rocks as they strained beneath the weight of overlying rocks, but many also record small movements that represent tiny earthquakes occurring over millions of years. Each time an earthquake is generated by movement along a fracture or fault in the Earth, it leaves behind a trace of its occurrence, like the scar from an injury to your body. Layers in the rocks have been displaced and offset by movements along the fractures: the amount of movement depends on the energy of the earthquake. Little earthquakes leave only little scars, but big earthquakes can leave large, almost permanent scars, which can be seen as long continuous lines in the surface of the land. As scars on our body remind us of some painful event in the past, the scars on the Earth can be read by geologists to tell when, where, and how big past earthquakes have been.

Small and medium-sized earthquakes don't have enough energy to create a visible fracture. In New Zealand, only earthquakes bigger than about magnitude 6.5 result in the formation of major cracks or large faults at the Earth's surface. These faults form during the short time when the Earth is shaking during the earthquake, and can be recognised as long, straight lines of broken and disturbed ground. Features such as streams or roads that were unbroken across the

*Cross-section of the Earth. Large-scale seismic waves can reverberate within the planet for months, as if it were a giant bell. Travel pathways (arrows) are reflected and refracted by major boundaries within the Earth. The direction and speed of the waves is largely determined by differences in density of the medium through which they travel.*

*(Te Papa)*

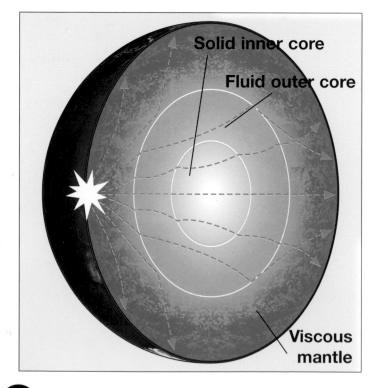

Solid inner core

Fluid outer core

Viscous mantle

Ohariu Fault

Wellington Fault

line of the fault before the earthquake can be offset as much as 10 metres (either vertically or sideways) when the Earth stops shaking.

Last century, a young geologist sent out to record the effects of the 1888 Glynn Wye Earthquake near Hanmer in North Canterbury was the first scientist in the world to recognise an association between major earthquakes and horizontal displacements of the ground surface. Alexander McKay, a geologist working for the New Zealand Geological Survey, mapped the earthquake fault trace of the Hope Fault for more than 30 kilometres, and in 1891 he published photographs and an explanation of how the earthquake had resulted in up to 2.5 metres of sideways movement of the land. His observations went largely unnoticed outside of New Zealand, but were supported when the great San Francisco Earthquake of 1906 resulted in an earthquake trace nearly 300 kilometres long and a maximum sideways displacement of nearly nine metres.

There are hundreds of faults throughout New Zealand. Many of these are close to our major cities. The Wellington Fault runs right through Wellington City, with the Wairarapa Fault passing nearby; the Akatore and Titri Faults are near Dunedin; Christchurch has the Amberley Fault, to the north; and Auckland has the Drury and Wairoa North Faults to the south-east of the city. Our mountain ranges are nearly always bounded by faults and contain many faults within them. The most famous of all is the Alpine Fault, which extends almost the whole length of the South Island, from Milford Sound to Cook Strait.

All these faults are of interest to geologists, who want to understand the formation and evolution of the rock masses that make up our land. Over many

*Wellington from the air. At this height the major faults stand out as lines through the landscape. The Ohariu Fault is to the west, the Wellington Fault runs through the city and along the western side of the harbour and Hutt Valley.*
(IGNS)

49

The South Island as viewed by a Space Shuttle astronaut from above Fiordland. The Alpine Fault is clearly visible as the sharp diagonal line highlighted by the edge of the snow-covered Southern Alps. (Landsat/NASA STS059229017)

Right: *This photograph of a repaired fence, taken by Alexander McKay, shows the movement along the Hope Fault in the 1888 earthquake near Glynn Wye. The fence was broken by the fault moving nearly 2.5 metres sideways.* (IGNS)

millions of years, the New Zealand landmass has continually been subjected to stresses and strains that have caused the Earth to bend and crack. Many of these faults have been active and generated large earthquakes in the geological past. Faults become inactive when the pattern of forces around them changes, and they are no longer acting in the places and at the correct orientation to generate earthquakes.

In New Zealand, geologists believe that if a fault shows evidence of having moved at least once in the last 125,000 years, then it should be considered to be a potential source of large earthquakes in the future. If it has moved at least once in the last 5,000 years, then it must be considered a potential source of damaging earthquakes to any settlement within a radius of 50 kilometres.

Land movements and the formation of fault scarps in association with large earthquakes have been observed in New Zealand at least 11 times since 1848. In all cases the movements have occurred in exactly the same place where there has been similar movement in the past (although in many cases this was recognised only after the earthquake revealed the fault's

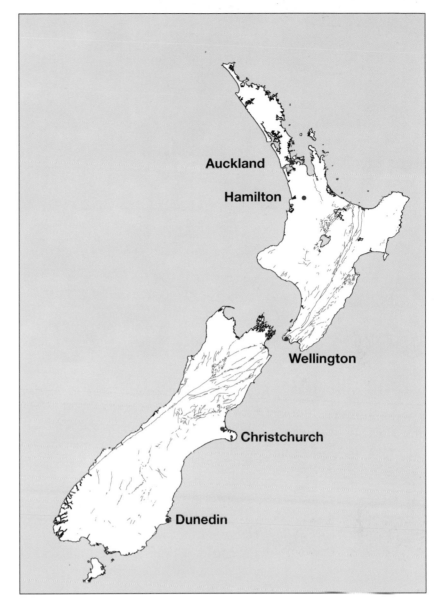

*Active faults of New Zealand. Each line represents a fault that has moved within the last 125,000 years.*
(IGNS)

location). Once a major fault has been formed, future earthquakes are generated along the same line, and after hundreds of thousands or millions of years of movement, increasingly large vertical and horizontal separations of the land can occur. Rocks that were once side by side have been displaced along the Alpine Fault, with one lot ending up in Nelson and the other nearly 500 kilometres away in Fiordland! Repeated earthquakes and their associated fault movements have formed the major mountain ranges of New Zealand and the mountains along the Alpine Fault of the central South Island.

Harold Wellman, who in the 1940s was the first geologist to recognise the phenomenon of similar rocks having been displaced along the Alpine Fault, also recognised that smaller-scale movements could be seen in the landscape. Together with Pat Suggate and Gerald Lensen of the New Zealand Geological Survey, he mapped most of the major faults in New Zealand during the 1950s and 1960s. The three geologists mapped the progressive offset of old abandoned river courses emerging from the mountains of central New Zealand, and showed that this movement could be used to calculate the rate at which the land was being shifted. They saw that for hundreds or even thousands of years the faults stayed

*Harold Wellman, surveyor and geologist (1909-99).*

(IGNS)

locked together, but when an earthquake occurred the land would shift sideways, in some cases as much as 13 metres. They reasoned that if they could determine the age of the old abandoned river course and the size of each earthquake movement, assuming that each movement was about the same size, they could calculate the average time between major earthquakes.

Twenty years later their ideas began to be tested by New Zealand geologists who started digging large trenches across these faultlines to try and date more precisely the timing of these past earthquakes. These trenches revealed layers of young soil and river deposits which had been offset vertically and horizontally by movements associated with prehistoric earthquakes. The older layers were offset more than the younger layers, and by careful use of radiocarbon dating methods the timing of individual earthquakes could be narrowed down. By this method the trenching studies established not only the average rates of movement for many faults, but also the average time between large earthquakes – and the time since the last one. This work has helped scientists to estimate the likelihood of future large earthquakes near cities like Wellington and Christchurch.

*The Wairarapa Fault scarp at Pigeon Bush. This locality records evidence of large movements during the last two big earthquakes on this fault. In each instance the scarp rose 6.5 metres vertically and moved sideways 13 metres! The old positions of the stream are clearly visible.*

(Rodney Grapes)

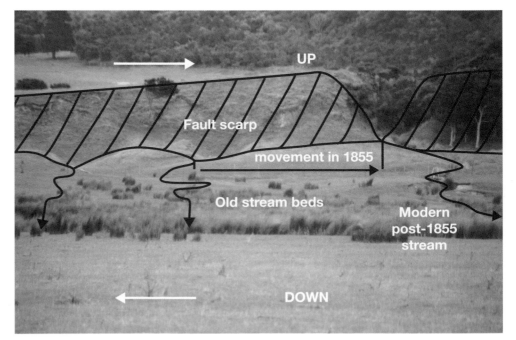

UP

Fault scarp

movement in 1855

Old stream beds

Modern post-1855 stream

DOWN

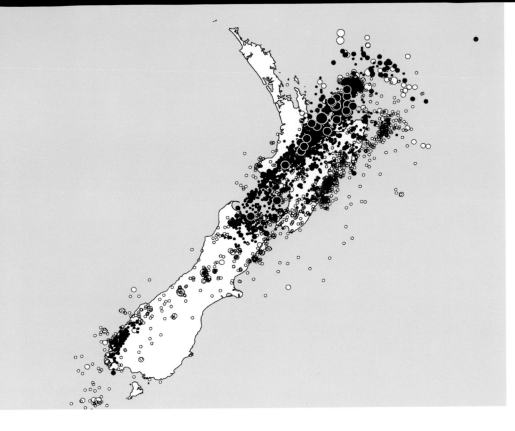

Many of New Zealand's earthquake faults occur under the sea, particularly along the East Coast of the North Island from Wellington to East Cape, and along the eastern coast of the northern South Island. When these faults move during earthquakes they cause the land to be suddenly uplifted, and when the earthquake uplift exceeds the normal tidal range, then the beaches and shore platforms become preserved above the erosive effects of waves. By radiocarbon dating the shells of shellfish that were killed because of their sudden emergence from the sea, geologists can determine the number and likely magnitude of earthquakes that have occurred along the parts of the coast where terraces are preserved. Like the studies from trenches, the emergent beaches can be used to establish the time between major earthquakes and the time since the last big earthquake.

On 23 January 1855, a big earthquake struck Wellington, lifting the coast to the east of Wellington City by some 6 metres. The Hawke's Bay Earthquake of 1931 caused nearly 2 metres of earthquake uplift at Napier. And these were just two of the 22 earthquakes that have caused uplift along the North Island's eastern coast over the last 2,500 years!

about 5000 years ago

about 330 BC

1855

present storm beach

*Cape Turakirae, at the southern end of the Rimutaka Range, near Wellington, showing former shorelines indicating earthquake uplift. The base of the cliff is dated at 5,000 years ago, the next ridge (closer to the sea) is dated at about 330 BC, and the conspicuous one between this and the present-day shoreline marks the beach uplifted 6.4 metres in 1855.*

*(IGNS)*

## Measuring the shakes

The first question asked by people who have just experienced shaking from an earthquake is usually, 'How big was that one?' There is no simple answer. The best we can say is, 'It depends!'

'How big?' can mean several different things. Do we want to know how much energy was released at the earthquake source, or what the strength or intensity of the earthquake shaking was where we felt it?

Imagine you are buying a light bulb at the supermarket. You usually choose a light bulb by its energy rating (measured in Watts). This tells you how much energy is used to generate light at its source in the bulb. This is what the Richter Magnitude of an earthquake tells us – the amount of energy released at the source not how much shaking occurred at any one place.

The classification of earthquake strength or intensity began long before there were modern instruments to measure the earthquake motion. In the middle of the nineteenth century, four earthquake intensity zones were developed by Robert Mallet, an Irish engineer who witnessed the damage from the Great Neapolitan Earthquake in central Italy in December 1857. His earthquake intensity (strength) damage zones ranged from almost total destruction to a zone of almost no damage. He mapped in detail both the damage to buildings and how the local people reported the earthquake shaking, joining zones of equal intensity of damage by lines he called 'isoseismals', rather like the isobar lines on a weather map. He could locate the approximate source of the earthquake, determine the way the damage diminished away from the source, and use this as a basis to estimate the relative size of the earthquake.

Mallet's way of mapping the damage proved such a successful way to measure the intensity of earthquakes that the method was refined, first with a 1-10-zone scale, and later by a 1-12-zone scale developed by the Italian seismologist Mercalli in the early twentieth century. Mercalli's scale was later modified to suit the different building standards in California, resulting finally in the Modified Mercalli scale (MM) that is still used today. The MM scale has been modified for use in New Zealand. Engineers and scientists in New Zealand have adapted it to New Zealand building and construction methods, and removed the upper two divisions because they have not been experienced in even the largest earthquakes in New Zealand.

The real value of the MM scale, and why it is still used today even when we have arrays of high-tech instruments to measure earthquakes, is that it measures the intensity of an earthquake as it is experienced by people, buildings, and the natural environment. Newspaper surveys of local residents, engineering reports on damaged buildings, and geologists' reports on the location and extent of landslides, ground collapse, and fault ruptures are all used to determine the location and most severe intensity of earthquake shaking. Intensity mapping is done to compare today's earthquakes with those that occurred before seismometers were in wide use, and provides valuable information for planners and engineers.

*These flat surfaces at Table Cape, Mahia Peninsula, are remnants of old beaches that have successively uplifted by movement on offshore faults. Four marine-cut terraces are preserved on the coastal plain, and six older terraces, also marine-cut, have been recognised in the higher standing, more deeply eroded land behind.*

(IGNS)

## I feel the Earth move...

If we want to measure how strong or intense the earthquake was where we experienced it, then knowing the amount of energy released at the source (the Richter Magnitude) is not enough – we also need to know how far away the earthquake occurred. To measure the strength of an earthquake, we need to have some way of measuring the shaking and associated damage away from the source. This is what the Modified Mercalli earthquake intensity scale does. To use the light bulb analogy, we want to know the intensity or strength of the light where we are sitting, (the Mercalli Intensity) not just how much energy is being used to generate the light (the Richter Magnitude).

A low wattage bulb will never be very bright, no matter how close we get to it, while a high wattage bulb will be very bright close up and quite bright even at some distance away. Similarly, small earthquakes will only cause damage close to their source, but large earthquakes will cause great damage close to the source, and significant damage further away.

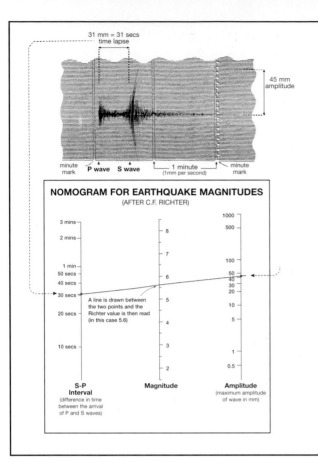

NOMOGRAM FOR EARTHQUAKE MAGNITUDES
(AFTER C.F. RICHTER)

A line is drawn between the two points and the Richter value is then read (in this case 5.6)

S-P Interval
(difference in time between the arrival of P and S waves)

Magnitude

Amplitude
(maximum amplitude of wave in mm)

Above: *The Richter magnitude of an earthquake is calculated using the height of the biggest wave and the time difference between the P and S waves.*
(Diagram by Salli Rowe, from Ansell and Taber *Caught in the Crunch*, HarperCollins, 1996)

Right: *Charles Richter, seismologist.*
(Archives of the California Institute of Technology)

As seismometers became more and more common and reliable in the early twentieth century, an American seismologist at the California Institute of Technology, Charles Richter, wondered how to measure the size of an earthquake without assessing all of the damage and talking to everyone who experienced it at different places. (The story goes that he undertook the development of the Richter Scale in response to constant questions from the media about how big the latest felt earthquake in California had been.)

Richter took his seismograph and measured the maximum amplitude (size) of the seismic trace on a seismogram from an earthquake 100 kilometres away. He found he could determine the distance to the earthquake based on the difference between the P and S wave arrival times. Because earthquakes vary a great deal in size he needed a scale that covered a wide range of measurements on his seismogram. Thus an earthquake 100 kilometres away that had a maximum deflection of the needle on his seismograph of 1 millimetre was defined as a magnitude 3 earthquake; one with a deflection of 10 centimetres as a magnitude 5. A magnitude 3 earthquake is therefore 100 times smaller than a magnitude 5 on the Richter scale.

Later studies showed that an increase in one Richter magnitude is not just 10 times bigger, but actually equal to about 30 times more energy released at the earthquake source deep in the Earth. That means a magnitude 7 earthquake releases nearly a million times more energy than a magnitude 3 earthquake!

The Richter scale proved to be very effective in quickly determining the size of an earthquake. People began to recognise that earthquakes less than about magnitude 5 did not cause any real damage, while earthquakes as big as magnitude 7 caused severe damage close to their source.

Seismologists in other countries had difficulty in getting exactly the same magnitude measurements as Charles Richter in California, but nevertheless they appreciated having a good measure of earthquake size that could be determined within minutes. Other magnitude scales have subsequently been developed that are independent of particular instruments or locations, and the Richter magnitude is now known by seismologists as 'local magnitude'. Seismologists now prefer to use a scale that directly relates the size of the earthquake to the energy released at the source, the moment magnitude scale. There are other magnitude scales related to measurement of the amplitudes of body waves and surface waves. This is why you often see slightly different magnitudes for the same earthquake, depending on which scale has been used.

Many people confuse the MM intensity scale and the Richter magnitude scale. Remember the light bulb. The Richter scale measures the energy rating, like the wattage rating on the light bulb. The Modified Mercalli scale measures intensity (how bright the light is where you are). The closer you are to the source, the greater the intensity.

## The bronze ball and the toad: detecting earthquakes

Devices for detecting earthquakes have been around for a long time. In the second century AD, Zhang Heng, a Chinese astronomer, mathematician, inventor, and geographer constructed the first known seismoscope (a simple form of seismometer). Although none of his original seismoscopes or plans exist today, detailed research in the late nineteenth century permitted the approximate structure of this first seismoscope to be determined. Zhang Heng's seismoscope consisted of a large bronze vessel three metres high and two metres in diameter, surrounded by eight large bronze toads aligned to the points of the compass. Many replicas of these instruments have been built in the last hundred years, but Te Papa contains the only one made in China for display in a foreign country.

Zhang Heng's seismoscope worked on the same basic principle used by modern electronic seismometers: a weight is suspended, and the amount it sways during an earthquake is closely monitored. In Zhang Heng's seismoscope, a heavy weight connected to the heads of eight dragons would move whenever earthquake shaking started. As the weight moved it opened the mouth of one of the dragons, releasing a brass ball that dropped into the waiting mouth of the bronze toad below. The toad that had

*Replica of Zhang Heng's seismoscope.*
(Awesome Forces exhibition, Te Papa)

*The distribution of the main seismometers used to detect earthquakes in New Zealand. The different colours show three different kinds of seismometers being used.*

(IGNS)

the ball indicated the direction from which the first earthquake waves had come.

The seismoscope is claimed to be very sensitive, detecting even very small earthquakes. Though we now know that the indicated direction of the earthquake would depend on whether it was the P or S waves that triggered the seismoscope, the device was very advanced in concept and construction – and remained so for the next eighteen hundred years!

Modern seismometers are complex electronic devices, although the basic principle remains the same. A weight is suspended on a spring and its movement is monitored very carefully. Seismometers are used in small and large arrays in earthquake-prone areas so that not only do they count the number of earthquakes, but they can also be used to locate the source of the earthquake and estimate the amount of energy released.

The first seismograph to detect earthquakes in New Zealand arrived in the early twentieth century. Although it was a sophisticated instrument for its time, it could really only count the number of earthquakes, rather than locate them. By 1964, a network of instruments was in place that could tell scientists the location and magnitude of the earthquakes occurring throughout New Zealand.

With continued advances in electronics, New Zealand seismologists have been able to design and build for themselves a digital seismograph network. By the early 1990s New Zealand had a network of 38 modern seismographs that could locate the 17,000 earthquakes that are detected each year. All earthquakes greater than magnitude 3.8 can be located accurately, while many smaller earthquakes occurring in the active volcanic region of the central North Island can also be pinpointed.

For all this shaking, only about a hundred or so of the 17,000 New Zealand earthquakes recorded each year are felt by people. The rest show up on seismographs. When large or damaging earthquakes occur, seismologists immediately deploy portable seismometers to record and locate all the small and moderate aftershocks that occur following a large earthquake. These sensitive instruments can record as many earthquakes in the space of two weeks as are recorded throughout New Zealand in a whole year. Detailed studies immediately after an earthquake are very useful for understanding the causes of earthquakes.

The Institute of Geological and Nuclear Sciences (IGNS) in Lower Hutt also maintains the National Strong Motion Network – an array of over 380 accelerometers (a special type of seismometer) that record earthquake accelerations. Unlike the seismometers that are working all of the time, these instruments only turn on when the shaking starts to reach a level that people can feel. After the earthquake, the data are downloaded by computer for analysis and interpretation by specially trained engineers. Records from these instruments help engineers understand how to strengthen old buildings and bridges and build new ones that will stand up to earthquake shaking during future earthquakes.

IGNS is now developing a new earthquake detection network that is capable of delivering information on the location, magnitude, and probable damage within minutes of an earthquake occurring anywhere in New Zealand. The network uses satellite communications and modern computer links. While the causes and unpredictability of earthquakes cannot be changed, the speed and appropriateness of our response can be improved dramatically by having high-quality, timely earthquake information on which to base our response.

## Great New Zealand earthquakes

Most New Zealanders have some personal experience of earthquakes. Yet the people living here last century probably had a greater awareness and sense of dread about the effects of an earthquake than we do today. The settlement of central New Zealand from the 1840s to 1860s coincided with a period of intense earthquake activity in the northern South Island and southern North Island. The largest known earthquake since Pākehā settlement occurred near Wellington in 1855, and followed damaging earthquakes in Wanganui in 1843 and Marlborough in 1848.

### 1855 Wairarapa Earthquake

On 23 January 1855 at 9.11 pm, the citizens of colonial New Zealand from Auckland to Dunedin experienced the shaking effects of a local magnitude 8.1-8.2 earthquake centred about 30 kilometres south-east of Wellington. While in Auckland and Dunedin this was just a minor rumble, people in small towns throughout central New Zealand saw buildings and the ground under them shake severely. In many places major damage resulted. From New Plymouth to just north of Christchurch chimneys and buildings were damaged, while as far away as Napier and Christchurch household items fell off shelves and were broken and damaged.

In Wellington, a town of 6,000 people, strong shaking lasted at least 50 seconds. All the chimneys collapsed, and most houses were damaged in some way. The newly built Government House and a local bank building were badly damaged. People were thrown to the ground by the shaking, and forced to lie in the broken remains of their furniture and possessions as everything tumbled around them. Although accurate records were not kept, as many as five to ten people may have been killed by collapsing buildings and landslides.

The earthquake generated a local tsunami over 10 metres high that swept both sides of Cook Strait (see Chapter 5 for the full story). In Wellington Harbour, a seiche (a sloshing oscillation, like tea sloshing when you jiggle a tea-cup)

Location and magnitude of
major earthquakes affecting
New Zealand since 1840.
(IGNS)

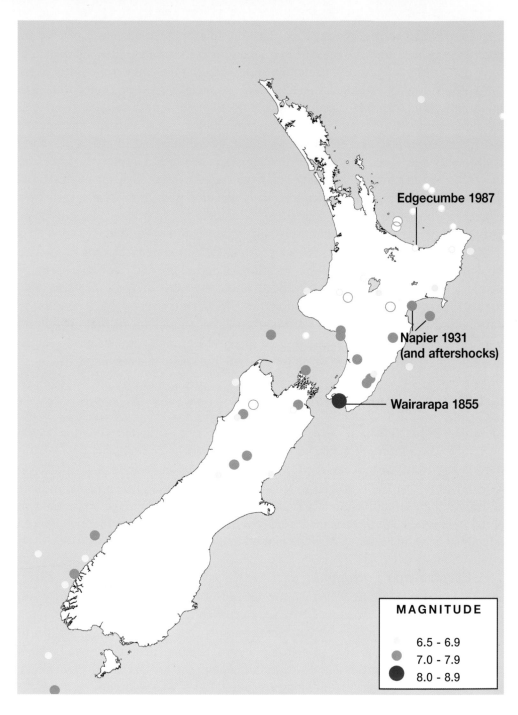

Edgecumbe 1987

Napier 1931
(and aftershocks)

Wairarapa 1855

**MAGNITUDE**

6.5 - 6.9

7.0 - 7.9

8.0 - 8.9

generated a wave about a metre high that flooded low-lying areas, and the waves continued to wash the shore every 20 minutes for the next 8-12 hours. Large numbers of bottom-dwelling, pressure-sensitive fish were killed by pressure changes caused by submarine landslides, and lay floating dead on the surface of Cook Strait. The tsunami also washed fish and debris above the storm tide line.

As well as having to confront their personal losses the next morning, people had to deal with hundreds of aftershocks greater than magnitude 5 that went on for several weeks. Constant smaller tremors were felt from the thousands of shocks around central New Zealand that exceeded magnitude 4. Indeed, some places felt aftershocks that were more severe than the main shock of 23 January.

When the next day dawned the landscape around the greater Wellington region had changed. Wellington Harbour was now 2.1 metres higher on the eastern side and about 1.2 metres higher on the west side. All the way from the Wairarapa to the west of Wellington the coast was fringed with a strip of new land uplifted out of the sea. Stranded fish and shellfish lay dead on this new land. The uplift reached its maximum of 6.4 metres near Turakirae Head to the east of Wellington Harbour, decreasing to no noticeable uplift on the west coast near Paekakariki. Some subsidence also occurred in the Wairarapa and in the Wairau Valley in the northern South Island. In all, some 5,000 square kilometres of land had been shifted vertically during the earthquake.

The Wairarapa Fault that bounded the east side of the ranges to the east of Wellington had moved, generating the earthquake. As well as causing uplift of much of the land on its west side, about 140 kilometres of the fault showed some horizontal displacement of features that were formerly continuous across it. The greatest lateral movement, from 9 to 13 metres, occurred along the line of the fault from the Cook Strait coast to about 70 kilometres north-east in the Wairarapa Valley. Horizontal and vertical movements decreased to the north-east to less than half a metre in the northern Wairarapa.

There was concern among the local citizens that the damaging effects of this and other early earthquakes would spoil Wellington's chances of becoming the capital. Newspapers and public meetings downplayed the earthquake's destructive side, stressing the benefits from the creation of new coastal land and the natural drainage of poorly-drained areas. As only one death was known to have occurred in the town of Wellington itself, the focus was on the reconstruction and creation of a modern urban area.

The cover-up was well done. It is only in recent years that scientists and engineers have come to understand that this earthquake is the largest recorded earthquake in New Zealand's short written history. On an international scale the 1855 earthquake is of major significance in terms of area affected, and the length and amount of fault movement.

*The raised shoreline along Lambton Quay, Wellington - the aftermath of the 1855 earthquake. Note the stranded jetties!*
(Photo taken by William Harding in 1860; Alexander Turnbull Library)

## 1931 Hawke's Bay Earthquake

The early 1920s were marked by a number of minor earthquakes that raised the level of awareness and concern about the potential effects of earthquakes. These fears were realised when in 1929 two earthquakes greater than local magnitude 7 occurred in central South Island – one in the sparsely populated Arthur's Pass region, and a more devastating magnitude 7.8 event near Murchison that resulted in 16 deaths and numerous landslides in the sparsely populated Buller District of the West Coast of the South Island.

Less than two years later New Zealanders were to learn what happens when a magnitude 7.8 earthquake makes a direct hit on an urban area. The Hawke's Bay Earthquake of 3 February 1931 is New Zealand's worst natural disaster to date, and the only time that an urban area has been devastated by a major earthquake.

The morning of 3 February 1931 was a typically warm, late summer morning in the pleasant climate of eastern Hawke's Bay. It was the first day back at school. The people of Napier and Hastings were going about their normal business. Under their feet, the Hawke Bay-Napier Fault had been accumulating strain, built up over thousands of years of slow compression between the Pacific and Australian plates. At 10.47 am the fault lost its ability to withstand the strain. About 20 kilometres below the surface and about 30 kilometres to the west of Napier the fault started to slip and unleash enormous energy into the near surface rocks of Hawke's Bay.

The shaking generated by this release of energy threw the residents of Hawke's Bay and the surrounding region into panic. The ground moved upward and sideways; the Earth's surface rippled like the surface of a pond as wave after wave heaved and rucked up the ground surface. People were thrown to the ground; buildings swayed and swayed until

they could stand the shaking no longer. Fountains of sand and mud erupted from beneath the surface of paddocks and streets; and anything that was not well secured was thrown to the ground. The shaking lasted for almost two terrifying minutes – an experience that was never to be forgotten by those who survived it.

When finally the severest of the shaking stopped, the town had been wrecked. Whole buildings had been shaken to a pile of rubble. Others were resting at strange angles or had large parts of their structures in tatters around them. Every house in Napier had been damaged in some way. Many had a toppled chimney and broken pipes, while others were buckled and broken as the ground underneath them had liquefied during the shaking. On Bluff Hill the new wing of the Nurses' Home had collapsed, killing eight sleeping nurses from the previous night's shift, and trapping

Top: *Downtown destruction: Napier's central business district after the earthquake and ensuing fires.* (Alexander Turnbull Library, Te Puna Mātauranga o Aotearoa; neg. no C-21789-1/2)

Left: *The Masonic Hotel, Napier, well alight!* (Collection of the Hawke's Bay Cultural Trust, Hawke's Bay Museum)

several more. Many of the older brick buildings were severely damaged, but the more recently constructed reinforced concrete buildings showed only minor structural damage, although their contents were in great disarray.

While the damage caused by the severest of the shaking was over, more tragedy was on its way. Small fires broke out and became raging infernos that were difficult to extinguish. Quick-thinking citizens were able to subdue the fires in Hastings, Wairoa, and Gisborne where the water supply was partially

functioning, but in Napier the water supply was ruptured and the streets so cluttered with rubble that fires could not easily be put out in the central business area. Fanned by onshore breezes, the fires burned virtually uncontrolled in Napier town for two days, gutting over 4 hectares of the business district. When the fires were finally put out and the missing people recovered from collapsed and damaged buildings, it was found that 256 people had died: 161 in Napier, 93 in Hastings, and 2 in Wairoa.

Once the citizens of Hawke's Bay had totted up their personal and property losses, they could start to measure the environmental impacts of the earthquake. Most noticeable were the changes to Ahuriri Lagoon and the Tutaekuri River that surrounded the town of Napier. The Tutaekuri River had changed its course southward by shifting permanently into what had been its overflow channel. This shift had been caused by uplift and tilting of the coastline. The coastal area to the north of Clive had been uplifted and tilted to the west, while the area to the south had subsided. The river could not flow uphill to the lagoon, so it shifted southward.

The west side of Ahuriri Lagoon had risen about a metre and the east side about two metres. Only about half of the former lagoon was now covered at high tide, and it was now too shallow to be navigable by even small boats. The new land was drained and the tidal parts of the lagoon dyked to prepare for new farmland and residential land surrounding Napier. In all a dome about 100 kilometres long and nearly 20 kilometres wide had been uplifted by a maximum of 2.7 metres during the earthquake shaking.

Napier and Hastings lay toward the southern end of the zone of earthquake uplift. The maximum uplift was near the mouth of the Mohaka River, halfway between Napier and Wairoa. While the uplift was not so apparent in the sparsely populated rural areas, some very large landslides had occurred along the coast. The biggest resulted in 80 hectares of land slumping into the sea. Another slumped across a river, pushing a 15 metre-high wall of water up the river and destroying the road bridge in its way. Numerous landslides also fell from Bluff Hill in Napier, undermining houses built near the hill's edge and blocking roads.

Top: *Dead fish in Ahuriri Lagoon, stranded after the sea retreated. The land was uplifted by one to two metres.*
(Napier Daily Telegraph)

*Searching for survivors buried in Napier's smoking ruins.*
(Alexander Turnbull Library, Te Puna Mātauranga o Aotearoa; neg. no F-20052-1/2)

## That uneasy feeling...

Models of the Hawke's Bay Earthquake movements suggest that it was caused by an average movement of about 8 metres vertically and 6 metres horizontally along the Hawke Bay-Napier Fault beneath coastal Hawke's Bay. Studies of the faults south of Hastings and studies of land movements within Ahuriri Lagoon show that earthquakes like that in 1931 probably occur about every 3,000-5,000 years. This does not mean that the inhabitants of Hawke's Bay can rest easy now that a big earthquake has happened, because there are at least another 20 faultlines similar to the one that moved in 1931 within 100 kilometres of Napier! Any one of them could move at any time, although the shaking will probably not be as severe as that devastating summer morning in 1931.

To the south of Hastings, the fault scars caused by the earthquakes were clearly visible. About 15 kilometres of fault trace were mapped several months after the earthquake, and can still be seen today.

The decade after the Hawke's Bay Earthquake saw a magnitude 6.9 earthquake in Wairoa in 1932, a magnitude 7.6 earthquake near Pahiatua in 1934, and two magnitude 7 earthquakes near Masterton in 1942. This sequence of large damaging earthquakes was an unequivocal message to people in the central North Island that they were living in a region of high earthquake hazard. Since that time we have greatly improved our earthquake-resistant construction methods and our disaster planning. Fortunately New Zealand hasn't experienced so many major earthquakes in such a short period since that time.

## 1987 Edgecumbe Earthquake

Late February 1987 was an unnerving time for residents of the Bay of Plenty towns of Edgecumbe and Kawerau. At times swarms of small, shallow earthquakes rattled their houses and workplaces every few hours. While causing little or no damage, they were a constant reminder that part of coastal Bay of Plenty lies within the Taupo Volcanic Zone – the zone with the highest rate of earthquake occurrence in New Zealand and one that contains most of New Zealand's active volcanoes. Because swarms of earthquakes occur somewhere in the volcanic region every year or so, the Bay of Plenty people have become used to them – though they are always aware of their destructive potential.

At about 1.30 pm on 2 March 1987 a large jolt was felt throughout coastal Bay of Plenty. This earthquake was larger than most of the previous swarm events,

*A pushover. An 80-tonne locomotive was toppled by the force of the Edgecumbe earthquake. The warped rails give a sense of the movement and energy unleashed.*
(Ross Land, courtesy of Fotopacific)

*Crumpled stainless steel milk silos at the Bay Milk Factory. (Whakatane Beacon)*

caused a power cut and alarmed people. In many cases they evacuated their workplaces, homes, and classrooms – a real earthquake drill! But just as they were beginning to think about going back inside, the local magnitude 6.3 main shock occurred as the ground beneath Edgecumbe let go its built-up strains.

The shaking jolted and shook everything in coastal Bay of Plenty. While this earthquake was only moderate by New Zealand standards, it was shallow (only 8 kilometres deep) and located close to the major towns of the region. There was significant damage. A paper-making machine weighing several tonnes jumped off its footing in the Tasman Pulp and Paper Mill. The milk in the tanks at the Bay Milk Factory sloshed violently from side to side, causing the tanks to rupture and spill their contents. The bridge over the Whakatane River had partly subsided and was unable to be used safely. Water pipes supplying Whakatane and outlying areas were damaged, as was the sewage pumping system, which was now pumping sand while sewage spilled from the broken pipes around it. The power supply was also severely disrupted. Residents were advised to stay at home and to conserve water and power until the emergency services could reconnect them.

Houses and small shops in the region were shaken severely, spilling their unsecured contents all over the floor. Many older houses shifted off their piles,

while others lost their chimneys and roofing tiles. Plumbing fixtures were broken or destroyed, causing water damage.

The earthquake had been generated by almost 3 metres of slip along the Edgecumbe Fault about 2 kilometres from the town of Edgecumbe. This previously unrecognised fault ruptured for 7 kilometres, creating a scarp up to 2.4 metres high and 1.6 metres wide. At McCracken Road the 1.5 metres wide fault scarp was somehow leapt by a Mini as its owner sped home. Several other faults around the Rangitaiki Plains also ruptured, although their length and amounts of displacement were much smaller than the main fault at Edgecumbe. Sand and mud fountains occurred close to the Edgecumbe Fault where the shaking was strongest, and also along the Whakatane River. Many landslides were triggered by shaking in the main earthquake and the magnitude 5.5 aftershock 10 minutes later. Tonnes of debris blocked the main and country roads, while clouds of dust from Whale Island, just offshore from Whakatane, signalled the collapse of part of the coastal cliffs.

Because of the moderate magnitude of the earthquake, the damage, while severe locally, was not widespread. Help was quickly on its way from Rotorua and further afield. Emergency services were able to meet most of the immediate needs of residents, and mercifully no one was killed, although many people were injured. Despite the moderate size of the earthquake, the insurance payout by the Earthquake Commission for houses and small businesses was nearly $136 million, making it New Zealand's most expensive earthquake event to date.

*Top left: The Edgecumbe Fault scarp intersecting McCracken Road. (IGNS)*

*Top right: The Rangitaiki River, with formerly submerged tree stumps standing proud. Movement on the Edgecumbe Fault lowered this area by up to 2.4 metres. During the earthquake, the river actually ran backwards! (IGNS)*

*The site of a sand fountain, caused by liquefaction during the Edgecumbe Earthquake. (IGNS)*

## Preparing for earthquakes

When people first arrived in this country, the atua (god) Ruaumoko writhed beneath the Earth to cause earthquakes, volcanoes, and geothermal steam. Fortunately, early Polynesian settlements were mostly in the north, where large earthquakes occur less frequently than in the centre of the country. Māori oral traditions of earthquake occurrence and their effects are not well explored, but we know that simply living here would have meant that their lives would have

*During the Edgecumbe
Earthquake Miss Harriet
Wubben's house became
instantaneously open plan. The
house was so badly damaged it
had to be demolished.*

(New Zealand Herald)

been affected by earthquakes.

With the arrival of Pākehā and construction of their settlements, the vulnerability to adverse earthquake effects grew. Immigrants from Britain were familiar with the building crafts of brick and mortar, and preferred to use this type of construction for larger and more important buildings. Wellington, Nelson, and Wanganui contained significant numbers of brick and stone buildings built in the British manner.

It was not long before these structures were found wanting. Partial or complete collapse of brick buildings led the early engineers and architects to develop a number of engineering innovations to make these buildings safer during moderate and frequent minor shaking.

In the early twentieth century, larger buildings were more frequently constructed with reinforced concrete, and to an informal code developed to accommodate the effects of moderate earthquakes. But when Napier and Hastings were flattened, engineers confirmed their views that concrete and brick buildings had to be better built. A code of engineering design followed from lessons learned from the building damage during the Hawke's Bay Earthquake. In the 1960s the Loadings Code became a mandatory standard, and it is regularly revised as our knowledge improves.

As well as developing sound codes of practice, New Zealand engineers have developed innovative devices to reduce the impact of strong earthquake shaking. From the 1960s, New Zealand research engineers developed and constructed devices attached to buildings and bridges to reduce the structural impact of earthquake shaking effects.

The most celebrated of these inventions is the lead-rubber bearing that isolates a building from its foundations, thereby permitting the ground to shake independently of the building. Invented by Dr Bill Robinson and his team of engineers at the former Department of Scientific and Industrial Research (now Industrial Research Limited), the base isolator device is now being used throughout the world to increase the resistance of important buildings to the effects of strong earthquake shaking. It has passed shaking tests in the laboratory and during major earthquakes in Japan and United States. One hundred and forty-two of these lead-rubber bearings isolate Te Papa from the earthquake-prone ground of Wellington. The building is just three kilometres from the Wellington Fault that will one day generate a major earthquake. Similar bearings have been used to reduce the potential earthquake damage to Parliament Buildings and the old Bank of New Zealand building, both in downtown Wellington.

Earthquake risk assessment has continued into the 1990s. Groups of scientists, engineers, utility operators, and city planners have combined their expertise to assess comprehensively the likely damage to Wellington's lifelines (water, gas, telecommunications, electricity, and roads) during the next major earthquake. Based on these assessments, city planners and lifeline operators have invested in measures to decrease the city's vulnerability to large earthquake shaking. Similar assessments have now been completed for Christchurch and Auckland, with new studies being undertaken in Hamilton, Hawke's Bay, Wairarapa, Timaru, and Dunedin.

## Ready for anything

New Zealand has developed a unique social response to the threat of earthquake damage. Following the repeated damage and personal losses from earthquakes occurring from the late 1920s to early 1940s, the New Zealand Government created the Earthquake and War Damage Commission (now the Earthquake Commission or EQC). This was a national insurance scheme that recognised that most New Zealanders had no cover for their losses from natural disasters, and some provision had to be made for the repair costs. Since 1945 the EQC has provided cover for all New Zealand homeowners against damage from earthquakes, volcanic and hydrothermal eruptions, landslides and tsunami.

Fortunately, there has not yet been a major call upon the fund, and EQC has accumulated large reserves to assist the reconstruction of New Zealanders' homes after a major natural disaster. EQC invests in most aspects of earthquake research – from locating faults to designing more resistant buildings – as well as actively promoting better community understanding of how to prepare and respond to an earthquake when it occurs. New Zealand's EQCover is a low-cost disaster insurance that is envied by many countries with similar natural hazard problems.

Earthquake building and design codes, lifelines engineering exercises, insurance provisions, and major revisions to New Zealand's emergency management procedures are all leading to a safer environment. However, our modern lifestyle and its dependence on a complex network of services and equipment make our livelihoods, if not our personal safety, more vulnerable to the sudden damaging effects of earthquakes.

One thing is clear. In the foreseeable future,

*A carving depicting the Maori god of earthquakes and volcanoes, Ruaumoko. (Awesome Forces exhibition, Te Papa)*

## Some recent large earthquakes

| Year | Date | Lat °S | Long °E | Depth (km)* | Magn. | Common name |
|------|------|--------|---------|-------------|-------|-------------|
| 1843 | Jul 8 | 39.9 | 175.0 | C | 7.5 | Wanganui |
| 1846 | Nov 18 | 41 | 172 | C | 6.5 | |
| 1848 | Oct 15 | 41.5 | 173.8 | S | 7.1 | Marlborough |
| 1853 | Jan 01 | 39.0 | 174.0 | C | 6.8 | |
| 1855 | Jan 23 | 41.4 | 175.0 | C | 8.1 | Wairarapa |
| 1863 | Feb 22 | 40.0 | 176.5 | C | 7.5 | |
| 1868 | Oct 18 | 40 | 173 | C | 7.0 | Cape Farewell |
| 1881 | Dec 04 | 42.6 | 172.3 | C | 6.8 | |
| 1888 | Aug 31 | 42.6 | 172.3 | C | 7.3 | North Canterbury |
| 1893 | Feb 11 | 40.8 | 174 | C | 7.2 | Nelson |
| 1895 | Aug 18 | 39 | 176 | C | 6.5 | Taupo |
| 1897 | Dec 07 | 40 | 175 | C | 7.0 | Wanganui |
| 1901 | Nov 15 | 43 | 173 | 12 | 6.9 | Cheviot |
| 1904 | Aug 08 | 40.6 | 177 | 30 | 6.7 | Cape Turnagain |
| 1914 | Oct 06 | 37.5 | 178.3 | S | 6.7 | East Cape I |
| | Oct 28 | 37.5 | 178.3 | S | 6.5 | East Cape II |
| 1917 | Aug 05 | 40.8 | 176 | <45? | 6.6 | |
| 1918 | Nov 03 | 47 | 165 | 50 | 6.8 | Puysegur Bank |
| 1927 | Feb 25 | 38 | 178 | 60 | 6.7 | |
| 1929 | Mar 09 | 42.8 | 171.9 | <15 | 7.1 | Arthur's Pass |
| 1929 | Jun 16 | 41.7 | 172.2 | 20 | 7.8 | Buller |
| 1931 | Feb 02 | 39.3 | 177 | 30 | 7.8 | Hawke's Bay |
| | Feb 13 | 39.5 | 177.5 | 30 | 7.3 | Hawke's Bay aftershock |
| 1932 | Sep 15 | 38.9 | 177.6 | 30 | 6.9 | Wairoa |
| 1934 | Mar 05 | 40.5 | 176.3 | 12R | 7.6 | Pahiatua |
| 1938 | Dec 16 | 45 | 167 | 60 | 7.0 | Charles Sound |
| 1939 | Feb 10 | 45 | 167 | C | 7 | |
| 1942 | Jun 24 | 40.9 | 175.9 | 15 | 7.2 | Wairarapa |
| | Aug 01 | 41.0 | 175.8 | 43 | 7.0 | Wairarapa |
| 1945 | Sep 01 | 47.5 | 166.1 | <45? | 7.0 | Puysegur Bank |
| 1968 | May 23 | 41.8 | 172.0 | 12R | 6.7 | Inangahua |
| 1976 | May 04 | 44.7 | 167.5 | 12R | 6.5 | Milford Sound |
| | Oct 12 | 46.7 | 166.0 | 12R | 6.5 | Puysegur Bank |
| 1993 | Aug 10 | 45.2 | 166.7 | 5R | 6.7 | Secretary Island |
| 1994 | Jun 18 | 43.0 | 171.5 | 11 | 6.7 | Arthur's Pass |
| 1995 | Feb 05 | 37.6 | 179.5 | 12R | 7.0 | East Cape |
| | Feb 10 | 37.9 | 179.5 | 12R | 6.5 | East Cape aftershock |

Shallow earthquakes (depth ≤ 70km), with local magnitudes greater than M 6.5, from 1840-1997.

*C: crustal (≤ 30km)

S: shallow

R depth restricted because of insufficient information

*Inventor of lead–rubber bearings, Bill Robinson (purple jersey) watches as four bearings are tested on a custom-built rig. These bearings have revolutionised building construction: some 142 bearings underpin Te Papa in Wellington.*
*(Penguin Engineering Limited)*

earthquakes will strike without warning, just as they have in the past. The results of more than 60 years of world-class earthquake research in New Zealand have permitted us to develop a society that can withstand the economic and social effects of a major earthquake. Better understanding of the causes and effects of earthquakes, and a determination to prepare for them in our personal and community lives, will reduce the risk of the inevitable next big earthquake turning into a disaster.

## Prepare for the worst

Make sure that your house is insured and covered by the provisions of EQCover. Older houses should be secured to their piles, dangerous loose chimneys taken down, unsecured hot-water cylinders strapped down, and all loose items on shelves should be secured. Know where your main gas and water taps are. Keep an emergency supply of food and fresh water on hand at home. Make an agreed response plan for each member of the family, so that everyone knows where to go and what to do when an earthquake strikes.

# Beware of falling rocks!

EILEEN AND MAURI MCSAVENEY

Just after midnight on 14 December 1991, a very loud rumble rattled Plateau Hut, startling climbers who were preparing to climb New Zealand's highest peak, Aoraki/Mount Cook, the next morning. Peering into the darkness, they saw bright orange flashes high up the mountain before the hut was enveloped in a cloud of dust. They all thought that the climb would have to be abandoned, as a mass of flowing rock and ice rubble, roaring like a mighty river in flood, swept across the Grand Plateau. The roar of the mountain falling continued for the rest of the night.

First light revealed the extent of the collapse. Twelve million cubic metres of the East Face of Aoraki/Mount Cook, including the summit, had gone. Sweeping across the ice of the Grand Plateau less than 300 metres from the hut, the rock debris had then cascaded down the steep Hochstetter Icefall and fanned out across the Tasman Glacier. The leading edge of the landslide crossed the two-kilometre wide glacier and stopped only after sloshing 70 metres up the other side of the valley. Other parts of the debris crossing the Grand Plateau rode 200 metres up slope to be launched from the crest of the ridge leading to Anzac Peaks before falling to the Tasman Glacier. The summit of Aoraki/Mount Cook was now trimmed to 3754 metres, its new highest point 14 metres south-west of the old summit. The former summit had plummeted down a seven-and-a-half kilometre path, dropping 2720 metres in the greatest fall possible in New Zealand.

No fatalities, no injuries, no property damage, but still the landslide made world headlines. A New Zealand national icon had irrevocably changed – Aoraki/Mount Cook was now 10 metres lower and looked different, but it was still our highest peak by a wide margin. (It is 257 metres higher than Mt Tasman, the second-highest peak.) Our fascination with the awesome forces of nature explains the headlines, but why did the peak fall?

The steep face had probably been ready to fall for a long time. Aoraki/Mount Cook is made of a sedimentary rock called greywacke – a kind of very hard

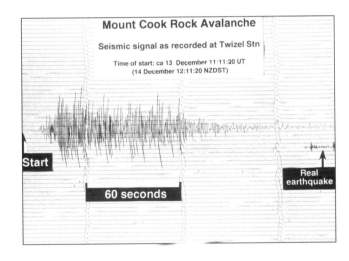

Mount Cook Rock Avalanche

Seismic signal as recorded at Twizel Stn

Time of start: ca 13 December 11·11:20 UT
(14 December 12:11:20 NZDST)

Start

60 seconds

Real earthquake

Opposite: *A national icon tumbles! In the greatest fall possible in New Zealand (2720 metres), the Aoraki/Mount Cook rock avalanche travelled 7.5 kilometres at an average speed of 200 kilometres an hour. Scouring snow and ice from its path, it reached the far side of the Tasman Glacier, dumping almost 29 million cubic metres of snow, ice, and rock rubble on the already debris-covered glacier.*
(IGNS)

*The earth moved to the beat of falling rocks from the collapse of Aoraki/Mount Cook, here recorded by a seismograph at Twizel 75 kilometres from the mountain, but also recorded in Wellington 500 kilometres away.*
(IGNS)

*Plumes of dust rise from the east face of Aoraki/Mount Cook as rocks continue to cascade from the unstable landslide scar, three days after the collapse. The black debris on the Grand Plateau (below) reveals how close the avalanche came to Plateau Hut (300 metres), before turning down the Hochstetter Icefall.*

*(IGNS)*

sandstone and mudstone – that is about 220 million years old. Although the rock inside the mountain, now exposed by the scar, is hard, it has been weakened by many fractures – it's a great pile of loose, shattered rock that New Zealand mountaineers call 'weetbix'. This large avalanche of rock from the Aoraki/Mount Cook massif was not the first. We know of other big rock-falls from the south-western flank in 1873, and from Mount Vancouver in 1974. And it certainly will not be the last: the upper slopes of the East Face of the peak are now steeper than ever. Some adjacent parts of the mountain that did not collapse also moved slightly – the Zubriggen Ridge leading to the summit dropped several metres, opening more cracks in the rock mass. The scene is already set for the next fall.

We know more about what didn't cause the collapse than about what did. There was no rain: the rock avalanche occurred on a clear, starlit night. No earthquake triggered it: instead, the collapsing mountain sent out its own distinctive tremors which were recorded on seismographs as far away as Wellington. The shaking peaked within 20 seconds, at the equivalent of a magnitude 3.9 earthquake, and continued for 70 seconds before dying away. Hours later a seismograph at Twizel, 75 kilometres away to the east, was still recording Aoraki/Mount Cook's falling rocks.

Earth forces are continually pushing this area of the Southern Alps upwards, adding about a centimetre a year to Aoraki/Mount Cook's height. The summit ridge is well protected from day-to-day erosion by a 10-metre thick carapace of very cold ice. The ice clinging to the steep flanks slowly moves downslope in the form of glaciers, plucking away the rock and undermining the peak. Inevitably, as time passes parts of the upper mountain surrender to gravity in the only way possible – by falling off!

The Aoraki/Mount Cook rock avalanche caused no damage, but this was a quirk of luck – had it fallen a few hours later, there would have been people in its path or on the summit. Had a section of the summit ridge closer to Aoraki/Mount Cook's Middle Peak collapsed, it would have been aimed at Plateau Hut instead of the Anzac Peaks ridge: the hut, and everyone inside, would have been obliterated in seconds.

Rock avalanches are extremely dangerous and dramatic, but they are the way gravity shapes mountain ridges. A rock avalanche bigger than one million cubic metres usually happens about every 30 years or so within the central Southern Alps. In 1991-92, however, we had three within a period of nine months!

# OK! So why do landslides fall?

Why landslides fall is a not a simple question to answer, because it involves two problems. First of all, we need to know what special conditions are needed to make a slope so unstable that a landslide is likely to occur. Secondly, we need to know what sort of events will tip the balance and finally trigger a landslide. Experts are still a long way from fully answering these questions for Aoraki/Mount Cook, or indeed for many of our large landslides. A fundamental difficulty with studying many types of landslides is that much of the critical evidence is destroyed in the moment of action.

Fractured, folded, and crushed by Earth forces, much of the rock of New Zealand is moving upwards, carrying the landscape higher and higher. Volcanoes also build up the land. They have added layers of lava and ash hundreds of metres thick to the central North Island. Opposing this upward growth are two equally relentless forces trying to level the land: climate and gravity. Rain and snow become rivers, streams, and glaciers that gnaw at the land, carrying rocks down to the sea. They carve their valleys ever deeper, but there is a limit to how high and how steep valley walls can become.

The natural slope of a valley's walls depends on the strength of the rocks that they are formed from. New Zealand's landscapes are underlain by rocks of many different types – some hard, some soft, some massively solid, some thinly layered. Crystalline rocks like granite that have formed far below the surface are often very strong. Many of the spectacular glacial valleys of Fiordland have been carved into strong rock of this type. In contrast, some soft rocks like shale, made of solidified clay, can be crumbled in your hand like flaky pastry – hills of such rock will quickly wear down to form only gentle slopes.

Any rock, no matter how strong, may weaken with the passage of time.

*The soft, weakly cemented sandstones of east-coast North Island form generally gentle slopes. Here, a fresh earthflow blocks Mangataikapua Stream west of Gisborne, in a landscape shaped mainly by landslides.*

(IGNS)

Exposed to water and air, even resistant rocks will in time be chemically altered, weathering down to soft clay minerals. Sedimentary rocks are made of layers of cemented grains – boulders, pebbles, sand, silt, and clay. The cement may slowly dissolve and the rock once again become loose sediment. Because all rock breaks down in time, in most places you rarely see it in its fresh state. The surface of the land is usually covered by soil, which is simply the weathered remains of the rock.

In high mountain areas, where temperatures can fluctuate above and below freezing, water is a powerful agent for breaking down rock into fragments. As water freezes and forms ice crystals, it expands. Crystallising water can exert tremendous pressure in a confined space. Put a plastic bottle of drink into the freezer to chill quickly, and then accidentally forget it, and you will later find the bottle in pieces – pushed apart by its expanding contents.

Mountaineers know that after a freezing-cold night, one of the most dangerous times of day to be climbing is when the morning sun first strikes the rock. During the night, rock fragments may split off from the cliff, pushed outward by growing ice crystals. Now stuck to the cliff by ice alone, the rocks become deadly missiles as the sun melts the ice and gravity takes its inevitable course. Likewise, falling rocks can play skittles with traffic on mountain roads when a thaw sets in.

No matter what type of rock a hill is made of, its ability to stay together in one piece is lessened by water from rain, melting ice, or leaking pipes, or by being shaken in an earthquake. A moment arrives when the force of gravity pulling the loosened and weathered rock down the hillslope is more than the strength of the rock can stand, and the mass moves downslope as a landslide. Gravity never lets

*The spectacularly steep slopes of Fiordland's glacially carved Clinton Valley are underlain by strong crystalline rock. But the area still has landslides triggered by rain and earthquakes.*

*(IGNS)*

up and inevitably wins out against even the strongest rock: all it has to do is wait to catch the rock in a weak moment.

The distinctive shapes of our high mountains are all sculptured by repeated episodic landslide collapses, as well as by rivers and glaciers. It is not just high mountains that are sculptured by landslides. To the experienced eye, many of New Zealand's hilly landscapes have a sagging look to them, and bear distinctive traces of landslide movement.

Landslides come in every shape and size. Most landslides are not as large, as fast, or as dramatic as the collapse of Aoraki/Mount Cook. Some are so slow that they move at about the same rate that your fingernails grow. These landslides are not a danger to anyone. A slowly moving landslide carries the North Island town of Te Puia Springs safely on its back. A number of New Zealand's highways cross slowly moving landslides, and require nothing more than occasional road resurfacing or realignment.

But most landslides are a danger to life, and are destructive to property. In 1995, the Earthquake Commission (EQC), which covers landslide damage to houses, paid out $3,590,872 for 'landslips'. To obtain the full cost to New Zealand of landslide damage for that year, we would have to add the costs of injuries to people hit by falling rocks, repairs to landslide-damaged roads, railways and other man-made works, and the cost of landslide damage to commercial properties including farm land. Not all of these damaging landslides were from natural causes: many occurred on steep roadside cuts, and some were triggered by leaking storm-water, sewer, and water pipes. Then of course there were the countless landslides which occurred naturally, well away from people and their property. Most of these passed unrecorded.

In New Zealand's brief recorded history we have had a surprisingly large number of landslide disasters. Some, such as the Abbotsford disaster, are caused by a single

On a landslide lubricated by hot water, the town of Te Puia Springs is on the move, diagonally towards the lower right. The landslide head is just beyond the town. The landslide is enormous. Only the slopes in the far background and extreme left foreground are not parts of it. (IGNS)

large landslide; other disasters, such as the landslides triggered by storms or earthquakes, may affect a whole region. Landslides severely compounded the damage caused by floods around Wellington in 1976, and around Gisborne during Cyclone Bola in 1986.

## Beware of falling rocks!

Only a few roads wend their way over the crest of the Southern Alps. Building the highways through these jagged, crumbling mountains presented a challenge to road builders, and maintaining them is an even greater challenge. In the Southern Alps, geology and climate combine to present one of the most destructive natural environments on the planet.

At first glance, the bottoms of the main valleys look promising. Filled with broad flat expanses of gravel threaded by innocuous shallow river channels, they form a low, gently sloping route into the heart of the mountains. These areas, however, flood frequently in mountain storms. To avoid flooding, the road must be made higher up, above the valley floors, and inside the zone where falling rocks have right of way, and use it frequently.

Natural hillsides have slope angles at which the bedrock is reasonably stable under normal conditions. Road builders disturb this stability by creating road-cuts. Cutting a notch into a hill undermines the slope, and it is not too surprising that cut slopes sometimes collapse.

In winter, the cycles of freeze and thaw send a steady supply of rock fragments downhill to build up mantles of scree on the mountain slopes. Mountain roads must commonly traverse these steeply sloping piles of loose

## Sand castles, beach towels, and water

A small child playing on a beach soon works out the basic rules of sand, water, and gravity. Fill your bucket with dry sand and turn it over, and you get only a boring pile of sand with low, sloping sides. Use damp sand, and you can build a proper sand castle with near-vertical walls. But if you add too much water to the sand, the soupy mixture simply flows away.

Water seeping into the land surface plays a Jekyll and Hyde role. A small amount of moisture dampens the soil and helps particles to adhere to each other. If it rains, however, water sinking into the soil gradually fills the openings between the grains. If rain continues until the soil is completely saturated, the water pressure in the soil increases, and may in time force the soil particles apart. Once the grains lose contact with each other, the saturated soil begins to flow.

Water plays another role, quite apart from bonding grains or lubricating them. Water adds weight. Sopping-wet beach towels and blankets, for example, are amazingly heavy compared to dry ones. Water-logged soil, wet plants, hail, and snow are all added weights that may tilt the balance between stability and instability, and cause a hill slope to fail.

rock. Removing rocks from the bottom of the pile invites an unwanted cascade of more rocks from above.

Mountain roads must also bridge innumerable streams coursing down the mountain sides. During storms, destructive flows of debris can form when landslides – even small ones – fall into steep torrents. These mixtures of rock and water reach the consistency of wet cement and can move with the speed and power of an express train. On steep slopes, they pick up everything in their path – trees, rocks, water – and grow quickly as they race downslope. Picturesque mountain brooks become immense, destructive debris flows, capable of burying people, buildings, and bridges, sometimes even of obliterating them without trace.

*Opposite: Landslides, landslides, and yet more landslides. Descending from Arthur's Pass, this section of State Highway 73, the Otira Zigzag, is built on the deposits of a series of prehistoric rock avalanches. The Otira River is undercutting the slope below the road – sections of the road drop out every 20 years or so. The scree slopes above the road are formed by rock falls that occasionally bombard road traffic. This section of road will be abandoned when a viaduct is built down the middle of the river.*
(IGNS)

*The remote high-country stations at the headwaters of the Rakaia River became even more isolated when this debris flow blocked their only access road after heavy rain.*
(IGNS)

# On shaky ground

*Shifted more than 50 metres from its original site, part of the upper story of the Morel homestead is all that remains of the Busch and Morel homesteads. Five people died when these houses were destroyed by a huge landslide in the Murchison Earthquake of 17 June 1929. The landslide raced 1.2 kilometres across the Matakitaki Flats and dammed the Matakitaki River about five kilometres south of Murchison, forming a temporary lake 5 kilometres long and up to 24 metres deep.*

*(Alexander Turnbull Library)*

Living as we do in a geologically active land, New Zealanders are aware of the ever-present possibility of earthquakes. People who live in the Wellington area, for example, take in their stride the tremors that rattle their homes and offices several times a year.

Our worst fear is that a powerful earthquake will strike a city: destroying buildings, bridges, elevated highways, and dams; breaking gas, water and sewer pipes. In a hilly and mountainous country such as New Zealand, however, earthquakes bring another danger – they trigger landslides.

During an earthquake, steep hills and mountain ridges focus and amplify the ground-shaking waves. This increases the chance of landslides from their upper slopes.

With a magnitude of 7.8, the 1929 Murchison (Buller) Earthquake was one of the more powerful earthquakes to occur in New Zealand this century. Centred in the rugged mountains of north-west Nelson, it was felt from Auckland to Dunedin. The earthquake struck in mid-winter, on 17 June 1929, a time when the hill slopes were heavily water-logged. The powerful tremors triggered countless small slips and at least 50 large landslides. Of the 17 people who perished in this quake, 14 were killed directly by landslides; while two men died in mine cave-ins. (The other fatality was a diabetic, who died from lack of access to essential medication – insulin.)

A number of rivers and streams, including the mighty Buller River, were temporarily dammed by slide debris during the Murchison Earthquake. Kilometres of roads vanished beneath tonnes of rock debris. Numerous landslides and rock falls on a 30-kilometre long stretch of the road to Karamea totally isolated the town. One resident walked 50 kilometres to Westport to try to get help. It was two weeks after the earthquake before a pilot was able to land his Tiger Moth on the Karamea beach, bringing some supplies. Nothing reached the town by road for several months. The road between Inangahua Junction and Murchison did not reopen until nearly two years after the earthquake.

Almost 40 years later, on 24 May 1968, the region was once again shaken, this time by a magnitude 7.1 earthquake centred near Inangahua, 35 kilometres west of Murchison. Once again, massive damage was caused by landslides. Two people died, both killed by a landslide, roads through the region took months to be cleared, and many rivers were blocked, including the Buller River.

New Zealand's most powerful earthquake since European settlement was the 1855 Wairarapa Earthquake. It tilted the entire Wellington region, raising the south-eastern end of the Rimutaka Range by at least 6.4 metres. The earthquake, estimated to have a magnitude of 8.2, triggered landslides over an area of 20,000 square kilometres, at distances of up to 300 kilometres from the earthquake's epicentre. A painting that now hangs in the Alexander Turnbull Library shows a large landslide from the scarp of the Wellington Fault that blocked the road from Wellington to the Hutt Valley. Most of the roads in hilly

One of the many landslides triggered by the 1968 Inangahua Earthquake destroyed a section of the Lower Buller Road and narrowly missed the hotel at Walkers Flat.
(IGNS)

Between Wellington and the Hutt Valley, State Highway 2 now crosses the foot of this 300,000 cubic metre landslide. It was one of many which fell around the southern North Island in 1855 during New Zealand's largest historical earthquake.
(Artist: Charles Gold, Alexander Turnbull Library; IGNS)

areas around Wellington were damaged by landslides. As much commuting then was done by 4-leg-drive horses, travel was not quite so inconvenienced by bits of missing road as it would be today. The 1855 earthquake had closely followed another damaging earthquake in 1848. Not surprisingly, a number of new immigrants promptly headed home to Britain, where only the economy was shaky!

# The world's second largest rock slide: Green Lake

Deep in Fiordland National Park, near Lake Monowai, lies one of New Zealand's best-kept secrets – the second largest landslide of its kind on the planet. A 9-kilometre long section of the crest of the Hunter Mountains has collapsed, dropping into the deep glacial valley of the Grebe River. The debris sprawls over an area of 45 square kilometres. Many large landslides are relatively thin, but the Green Lake landslide (named for the lake which sits on one corner) fills the valley to a depth of 800 metres – some 27 cubic kilometres of rock debris in all.

Green Lake landslide was discovered in 1976 by geologist Roger McPherson, who was looking at aerial photographs of the Lake Monowai area. How could something that big remain unrecognised for so long?

The landslide is well camouflaged and very old. It occurred long before any people, Māori or European, lived here – probably 12,000 to 13,000 years ago. Both the scar of the landslide and the rock debris are totally smothered in the lush greenery of Fiordland rain forest. From the ground, its most effective disguise is its sheer size – explorers, trampers (even geologists!) wandering through the low-lying forested maze of small hills and lakes never guessed that they were traversing a vast landslide.

What could trigger a landslide of that size? Fiordland is noted for the heavy rains that deluge the landscape almost daily, but mere rain is not enough to bring down such a massive section of mountain range.

The landslide occurred at the end of the last Ice Age, when the huge glacier that had once flowed through Grebe Valley into Lake Monowai had retreated far up the valley toward Lake Manapouri. Erosion by ice had left the valley walls that flanked the Hunter Mountains steep – perhaps too steep. It is likely that only a powerful earthquake, of a magnitude of at least 7.5 (and probably greater), could have shaken loose a section of the range.

Geologists have found that the landslide broke away along a fault zone, the Mt Cuthbert Fault. The range crest slid downslope on the crushed and weakened rock of the fault. The landslide, however, may not have been triggered by movement along the Mt Cuthbert Fault itself.

Seventy-five kilo-metres north-west of the Green Lake landslide is New Zealand's great

Alpine Fault. No mere local fracture, the Alpine Fault is a planet-scale boundary – the meeting place between two huge moving plates of the Earth's crust. When these plates shift, they generate powerful and destructive earthquakes. The Hunter Mountains may have been laid low by movement on the Alpine Fault – a catastrophic earthquake to cause a catastrophic landslide.

## Immense landslides in the making

Big strato-volcanoes such as Ruapehu and Taranaki have built into their structure all the essentials for creating huge landslides. Over the millennia, steeply sloping cones of lava flows alternating with loose ash and greasy soil have built up. Rain and melting snow fill the pores of the ash layers with ground water. Shaken and stirred during repeated eruptions, the fractured rock masses in these volcanoes are under the constant tug of gravity – immense landslides just waiting to happen. We know this because the plains that ring these volcanoes abound with the geological evidence of similar great landslides in the past. At long intervals in their history, usually when they are being disturbed and inflated by the intrusion of fresh magma, whole sectors of their volcanic edifices have collapsed, sending several

*The 'ring plain' around Mount Taranaki. The mountain has a complex history of cone-building episodes followed by cone collapse episodes when much of the volcano is destroyed, creating large avalanches (lahars) of rock and sediment that bury the surrounding countryside. The mounds you see in the foreground represent large rock fragments laid down by an avalanche formed from a cone collapse. Although Mt Taranaki is around 130,000 years old, most of the cone we see today is only about 70,000 years old, and has rapidly built up since the last major collapse. (IGNS)*

*The 250-metre deep Lake Waikaremoana formed 2,200 years ago when an earthquake shook a huge wedge of sandstone and siltstone nearly three kilometres long from the western end of the Ngamoko Range to block the Waikaretaheke River.*
(IGNS)

cubic kilometres of volcanic rock rubble out over their ring plains to form very distinctive landscapes of lahar mounds, and characteristic deposits of very highly fractured rock. We are fortunate that these are very rare events, for the danger zone for such collapses extends out to more than 75 kilometres from the source.

## Lakes dammed by landslides

When a large landslide falls into a valley, it may completely block the flow of a river or stream. Water will then pond upstream of the landslide, forming a lake. Such lakes are often a danger to communities downstream, since most dams formed by landslides are quite ephemeral, seldom lasting more than a few days. When the lake level rises and water begins to spill over the loose debris of the landslide, the water can rapidly erode the dam, spilling ever-increasing amounts of water and eroding ever more quickly. In a few moments, all the water of the lake may be let loose, creating a catastrophic flash-flood sweeping down the valley.

After the 1929 Murchison Earthquake, the small town of Seddonville was badly damaged by water and debris from the Karamea River when a landslide dam burst.

Not all landslide-dammed lakes are temporary. In the heart of Urewera National Park lies Waikaremoana. This lake formed a little over 2,000 years ago when a huge landslide, probably triggered by an earthquake, blocked the Waikaretaheke River. This landslide will not be easily eroded – it includes many huge blocks of rock, including a sandstone block nearly three kilometres long and a kilometre across. Instead of spilling over the top of the landslide deposit, the water of Waikaremoana leaks through the underground passages honeycombing the rocky interior of the landslide.

# Splash!

For many New Zealanders the ultimate dream is a home overlooking the ocean. Cliff-top houses with uninterrupted sea vistas command premium prices – and the stability of the site is seldom a consideration. New Zealand's coast is probably one of our most rapidly changing landscapes. Sea cliffs are under constant attack as waves smash against their feet. When they become undermined, they collapse in landslides.

Landslides also can fall into lakes and create waves. In May, and again in August of 1992, successive large rock avalanches from the crumbling flanks of Mount Fletcher, in the head-waters of Lake Tekapo, fell into Maud Lake. The first, larger rock avalanche sent a wall of water at least 10 metres high out of the lake into the Godley River. Nearly 8 million cubic metres of water flooded downstream into Lake Tekapo. The second rock avalanche fell onto an ice-covered lake, and the flood wave trimmed snow up to 7 metres above the lake shore. About 5 million cubic metres of water were ejected from Maud Lake by this smaller collapse.

*After torrential rain in 1979, seven landslides fell from cliffs at Omokoroa overlooking Tauranga Harbour. The most spectacular one fell from this 40-metre high cliff near Bramley Drive. Three homes above the headscarp were removed. The landslide created waves a metre high in the harbour.*

(IGNS)

## Landslide disasters at Waihi

In terms of the number of lives lost, New Zealand's worst recorded landslide disaster was in May 1846, on the south-western shore of Lake Taupo near the present-day village of Waihi. The Māori village of Te Rapa, home of chief Te Heu Heu and his tribe, was wiped out by the collapse of a landslide dam. An account of the disaster is recounted by a missionary, the Reverend Richard Taylor, in his book *Te Ika a Maui*, published in 1855:

> *In May 1846, a remarkable accident . . . terminated the life of this Chief, as well as the lives of his wives, and all of his children who were then living with him, together with nearly sixty of his tribe. An unusually rainy season occasioned a large land slip on the side of the Kakaramea, the mountain at the back of the Rapa, about two miles distance from his residence. This took place nearly 2,000 feet above the level of the lake, at the gorge of a little Alpine valley, through which a considerable stream flowed, which, being thus dammed up, in three days formed a large and deep lake, which burst its barriers, and, with irresistible force, swept rocks, trees and earth with it into the lake. The little settlement was buried with all its inhabitants, excepting a few solitary individuals, who, aroused from their sleep by the warning roar of the approaching avalanche, fled to the neighbouring hills, and escaped.*

In the second edition of his book, Reverend Taylor added:

> *There are traditions of two previous landslips in the same neighboured, one at Opotuka, when a hundred persons with their houses and fences disappeared in Rotaira Lake, the other at Omohu, a pa near Tokaanu not far from Te Rapa, when the pa, with one hundred and forty souls in it, was swallowed up.*

Eventually, a new Māori village, Waihi, was built near the site of Te Rapa, but chosen to be clear of any potential avalanche path. The site of the disaster was turned into fields used for growing kumara and corn. On 20 March 1910, at about nine in the morning, a sound like cannon-fire was heard, and the people of Waihi rushed outside. Looking up the Waimatai Valley, above the village, they saw a cloud of dust, like steam, rise in the air. First several slips gave way, then a 600-metre long section of fault scarp flanking the valley collapsed. Bush, rock, and soil plunged about 150 metres into the narrow valley, then shot down toward Waihi on the lowland at the lake edge. The people fled toward higher ground, but one man was overwhelmed by the landslide.

Emerging from the valley, the landslide poured across fields and crops, swept away houses and livestock, and spread out into Lake Taupo. It created a wave about 3 metres high that moved across to the opposite shore of the southern bay and swept children playing there off their feet; they were rescued by adults nearby.

The 1910 landslide took almost the same track as the 1846 slide that destroyed Te Rapa, but it was on a much larger scale. The earlier landslide was a mud flow, but the 1910 landslide was not caused by rain. Along the shores of Lake Taupo are many active thermal areas. Puffs of steam hang over the hundreds of boiling springs and steam vents on the hills behind Waihi. The volcanic rock of the area has been altered by the acidic water and gases, decomposing to soft, multi-coloured clays. The altered material is very much weaker than the original rock. As the disaster began with a loud noise and a cloud of steam or dust, the landslide may have been triggered by a hydrothermal eruption. A small slip may have occurred, releasing pressure and allowing water at high temperatures to flash to steam and explode, bringing down the hillside.

The land, proven unsafe for habitation in 1846, and abandoned as a village site, now was proven unsafe for cropping, and so it was sold.

## When more than rain falls...

Each year, from December to April, the warm equatorial oceans of the western Pacific spawn powerful tropical storms. Those that affect New Zealand form in the seas near Fiji, then follow a curving track southward. Most cyclones pass well to the north of us, but a few follow paths that bring them to New Zealand.

As these storms leave the tropics and encounter the cooler oceans around New Zealand, they lose some of their strength. By the time they reach here, their winds have weakened from hurricane force to gales, but the swirling warm air masses still contain vast amounts of water.

In March 1988, Cyclone Bola descended upon northern New Zealand, then became slow moving. Strong winds blew moist air and a thick sheet of clouds against the hills between East Cape and Gisborne, bringing days of continuous heavy rain. Up to 900 millimetres of rain fell in only three days, deluging the steep, easily eroded hill country.

Because of its soft bedrock, the East Cape-Gisborne area has always been more prone to landslide erosion than areas on more resistant rock. Through the millennia, however, the hillsides were sheltered from the onslaught of torrential rain by a natural umbrella – the forest canopy. Some of the rain that fell never reached the ground – it was intercepted by a myriad of leaves and simply evaporated back into the air. The lush vegetation and thick leaf litter on the forest

*This area south-west of Gisborne was hardest hit by landsliding in Cyclone Bola. (Courtesy Landcare Research)*

floor shielded the soil below from the impact of driving rain, and the tangled network of roots helped to hold the soft soil together. From the 1880s onward, however, that protection disappeared as European settlers cleared the forest.

Cyclone Bola rain fell on steep hills clothed largely in grass. As rain filled the space between the soil particles and water pressure built up, the upper layers of

### Tarndale Slip

One of New Zealand's more infamous patches of eroding countryside is in the hills north of Gisborne – the 'Tarndale slip'. Once a single narrow gully in a pasture back in 1915, the 'slip' now covers over 50 hectares. A belated program of tree-planting has slowed erosion in neighbouring small streams, but the main slip continues to eat into the soft rock of the hillside. With every heavy rain a slurry of rock debris pours into the Weraroa River below – since the turn of the century the river bed has risen some 25 metres. (IGNS)

soil separated and the sodden mass slid down the slopes.

As the slips multiplied, they exposed huge areas of bare ground to the driving rain – both the slip scars higher up the hillside, and the masses of churned-up pasture that had oozed downslope. Vast quantities of sediment were sluiced down the hillsides from the slips into streams, and from there into the rivers of the region. During Cyclone Bola, a million tonnes of sediment poured into the Waipaoa River from just one catchment with an area of 11,000 hectares – more sediment than had been washed out in the previous 15 years.

Some hill-country farms lost up to 30 per cent of their usable grazing land, along with fences, tracks, and drinking water for stock. The damage to hill country farms was estimated to total $15.6 million, with a further $3 million each year over the next 20 years because the eroded land was no longer as productive.

As rivers rose, they spilled over their banks, and muddy water spread over adjacent farmland. Livestock drowned, and farmers lost crops, including grapes, squash, sweet corn, and tomatoes. The regional economy was estimated to have lost $30 to $40 million.

It is not just wayward tropical cyclones that bring heavy rain to New Zealand. Our location in the Roaring Forties ensures us a prodigious supply of rain. No town in New Zealand is without its stories of the day when the heavens opened up. And if the town has a hill, the legends include the accompanying landsliding. Wellington City and the Hutt Valley are no exception. April to October 1974 was abysmally wet in the wettest year on record for Wellington. With no one particularly bad storm, it still was a bad year for slipping – 1149 landslips were recorded within Wellington City. Most were on

*Cyclone Bola triggered large landslides as well as small ones. This one has dammed a stream, creating a lake filled with muddy floodwater.*
(Courtesy Landcare Research)

slopes cut for roads, houses, sports fields, and schools; only two were on natural slopes. The slips ranged in volume from less than a cubic metre to 9500 cubic metres.

Residents of Ngahere Street, Stokes Valley have good reason to recall the storm in the Wellington area on 20 December 1976. Exceptionally heavy rain, more than 350 millimetres falling in 24 hours around Belmont, caused widespread flooding and landslides in Wellington City and the Hutt Valley. One landslide took out three houses in one street.

## Landslides in slow motion: Central Otago

In the 1970s, the prospect of electricity shortages in New Zealand loomed large. The solution was seen to be yet another dam in the South Island – the Clyde Dam on the Clutha River in Central Otago. The dam would be built near the town of Clyde, and would back up water through the Cromwell Gorge, where the river flows through the mountains between the towns of Cromwell and Clyde.

Upstream of the dam, the mountain slopes above the Clutha River have a strange appearance. Rain is infrequent in the semi-arid climate, and few stream channels or gullies drain the hillsides. Instead the valley walls are covered in humps and hollows, giving them a curiously rippled appearance.

The mountains of Central Otago are made of a soft, highly deformed rock

*Three homes in Ngahere Street in Stokes Valley, a suburb of Hutt City, were destroyed by a landslide during the torrential rain of 20 December 1976.*
(Evening Post)

called schist. The Clutha River had carved a deep gorge through the schist, and now the valley walls were responding to gravity. They were sagging, creeping slowly downslope millimetre by millimetre. That meant that the walls of long sections of the valley above the dam consisted of landslides – but landslides moving in ultra-slow motion.

Engineers were worried. Although the hillsides were creeping along at a barely perceptible rate, it was always possible that they might suddenly give way. As water rose behind the dam to form the new reservoir, Lake Dunstan, the bases of the many landslides would be immersed under as much as 60 metres of water. After the lake water had weakened the toes of the hillsides, any disturbances in the area, such as a storm or minor earthquake, might trigger sudden rapid movement. A section of hillside plunging into the lake would create massive waves that could overtop the Clyde Dam. Even if the dam weren't damaged, the water sweeping over it would swamp the small town of Clyde, just downstream.

For safety, the hillsides had to be stabilised. Knowing that high levels of groundwater make hillsides less stable, engineers decided that one solution was to drain the land. They drove long sloping shafts into the valley walls. Central Otago has very low rainfall – it is one of the driest areas in New Zealand. The landslides were expected to contain some water, but few were prepared for the quantities that gushed from the drainage shafts. The creeping landslides were indeed being

lubricated by water – large amounts of it under high pressure. Eventually, at great expense, over 14.5 kilometres of tunnels were excavated. From this network of tunnels, more than 78 kilometres of drainage holes were then drilled, fanning out into the slides to drain them permanently.

A second, and equally expensive, way to stabilise some of the landslides involved a massive re-arrangement of the landscape. One way to keep a hillside from sliding down is to block its movement by placing a large weight of material on its toes. An army of bulldozers and earthmoving machines began piling up and compacting rock and earth at the feet of the most active landslides. By the end of the project more than five million cubic metres of material had been shifted to create vast earth buttresses.

One troublesome landslide, the Cairnmuir slide, threatened to tumble over a cliff into the lake, and continued to move despite all attempts to drain the water out. Movement picked up each time it rained. The solution to stabilising this landslide was to stop water getting in. The landslide surface is now paved, and

*The slowly creeping landslides lining the slopes of the Cromwell Gorge are at least as stable now that Lake Dunstan is full as they were before the lake was created, because huge quantities of water once stored in them under high pressure have been drained. In often difficult working conditions of soft ground, loose rock, and copious water, tunnels were driven deeply into the hillsides, and from them, holes were drilled up into the landslides to drain them. (ECNZ)*

surface drains divert the rainwater before it has a chance to sink in.

By the time the Clyde Dam was complete, the work to keep these landslides in slow motion had cost $800 million, but it ensured the safety of a $2 billion power project.

*A close-up of some of the*
*damaged houses at Abbotsford.*
(Don Bird, Courtesy EQC)

## Nightmare in suburbia: Abbotsford Landslide

In the years following World War II, the suburb of Abbotsford spread across the gently-sloping spur of a hill on the western edge of Dunedin. It was a pleasant place to live, but from 1968 onward several families were plagued by a recurring problem. Annoying hairline cracks were appearing in their homes, zigzagging along the brickwork or across concrete floors and driveways.

On 30 May 1979 a leaking water main provided the first hint of escalating trouble. Workmen found that it hadn't broken: it had been pulled apart! Worried local authorities called geologists in to study the problem.

The hillside under Abbotsford is made of gently tilted layers of sedimentary rock. Known to geologists as the Abbotsford Formation, the layers were made of mudstone – a cemented mixture of sand, silt, and clay. On top of this bedrock is a ten-metre thick layer of compact sand, topped off with a thin cap of bouldery gravel and fine wind-blown silt. The key to the problem lay within the hillside, about ten metres below the surface. There, near the very top of the Abbotsford Formation, were some thin but treacherous layers of clay.

Water had been entering these layers and

the clay was becoming softer and more malleable, rather like children's modelling clay. The ground above it was beginning to shift, creeping imperceptibly down on an increasingly slick clay layer. The geologists were aware that landslides had occurred in other areas of Dunedin built on this type of bedrock. Ominously, the subdued shapes of several ancient landslides were visible at the foot of the Abbotsford hillside.

In the weeks that followed, two cracks, several dozen metres apart and roughly parallel to each other,

opened in long curves across the hillside pastures and through the eastern end of the suburb. Several streets of houses were now on the downhill side of the cracks. As the two cracks widened, the narrow block of land between them began to drop, creating a trough-like depression. Families whose homes straddled the cracks became the first victims of the developing disaster. As parts of their yard dropped away from under the foundations, their houses began to fracture, then crumple. By 1 July the first house in Abbotsford was evacuated, and more were abandoned in the following weeks.

For two months, millimetre by millimetre, the cracks became larger and longer, the trough of land between them sank lower, and the block of streets isolated by the cracks crept slowly downhill. Council workers fought a losing battle to keep the moving section of suburb liveable – patching fissures in the streets, bridging the steadily deepening trough, repairing ruptured water mains and sewer lines, and replacing electricity and telephone lines as they stretched to breaking point.

On 6 August, a civil defence emergency was declared. Residents were told to evacuate, but it wasn't considered urgent. Geologists felt that the slide would simply continue its stately progress, which by early August was nearly 150 millimetres each day. So on the evening of 9 August a number of people were still in the area, some packing and loading their belongings. A few minutes after 9pm, with a loud rumble, Abbotsford fell apart.

A seven-hectare block of hillside, bearing its consignment of streets and houses, headed downslope, miraculously intact. Seventeen people found themselves marooned on a moving island, gliding downhill at over three metres a minute. A deep gap opened on the uphill side of the moving block. Chunks of land, including the original sunken area between the cracks, collapsed with dull thuds into the growing rift. Much noisier were the sounds made by houses, luckily long since evacuated, splintering as they broke up and toppled in.

Within about 15 minutes the slide was largely over. The 17 men, women and children found themselves cut off from the rest of the suburb by a chasm 30 metres deep. A rescue team was organised, and two hours later they led the stranded people to safety, picking their way through the torn ground at the narrowest part of the gap.

Miraculously, no one was killed, or even badly hurt. Twenty-one houses had ended as shattered wreckage at the bottom of the chasm; several more teetering on the brink were later pushed over the edge to join them for an unceremonious bulldozer burial. The moving block of land looked solid when it came to rest, but was in fact riddled with cracks. Many of the houses there that had apparently survived the descent were structurally damaged beyond repair. In all, 69 Abbotsford homes were destroyed or rendered uninhabitable.

A Commission of Inquiry was instituted to study the Abbotsford landslide, and to answer an important question – was the disaster the result of natural causes alone, or was it, at least in part, the result of people's activities in the area?

The bedrock of the area was obviously prone to landsliding, but the landslides at the foot of the Abbotsford hillside were many thousands of years old. What had triggered the latest movement? Earthquake records showed no obvious seismic activity in the period before the hillside began to crack. The last earthquake that had shaken the Dunedin area hard enough to possibly affect the stability of the hillside had occurred in 1974, some five years earlier.

Harrison's Pit, a large quarry, had been excavated into the foot of the Abbotsford hillside between 1939 and 1969. Engineers suggested that removing

material there had made the hillslope slightly less stable, perhaps enough to tip the balance.

High ground-water levels could contribute to sliding. Weather records showed that the decade prior to the landslide had been wetter than average, but equally rainy periods had occurred in the 1900s and 1940s, with no ground movement. However, a Dunedin City Council water main through the Abbotsford area may have leaked slightly, adding to the high ground water and making the slope slightly less stable. Water lost as pipes broke during the early stages of land movement probably sped up the slide, but didn't start it.

In the end, frustratingly, no single factor could be assigned as the cause of the Abbotsford disaster – man and nature had each had a hand.

## Landslides and society: where to from here?

If you live and travel in New Zealand, you can't easily avoid the risk of being injured by a landslide. To leave Wellington via the Hutt Valley, for example, you cross the runout paths of many future landslides, since State Highway 2 traverses the foot of the scarp of the Wellington Fault. The scarp owes its broad outline to movement of the fault, but its detail has been sculptured by infrequent landslides.

With a surfeit of steep slopes, rocks, and rain, and no escape from earthquakes and the tug of gravity, New Zealand will continue to experience spectacular world-class landslides. We build around slopes – we often have little other choice – believing that the risk of people being hurt is outweighed by the benefits to the local society. However, societies, technical knowledge, and slopes exposed to the weather, all change with time. We should revisit, discuss, and reassess our decisions occasionally, lest the risks be forgotten.

# TSUNAMI

## The last wave

WILLEM DE LANGE

> There's a tsunami on the way.
> It's 70 metres high and travelling at 800 kph.
> Quick, are you insured?

So said an EQC advertising campaign of the late 1980s, designed to highlight natural hazards and the need for people to take out individual disaster insurance. The advertisement was based on the common understanding of tsunami: a very large, fast, breaking wave bearing down on the coast and sweeping all before it. But just how realistic is this picture of tsunami hazard for New Zealand?

## What is a tsunami?

A tsunami is a sequence of extremely long travelling waves, generated by large disturbances below or near the ocean floor. Tsunami travel fast, and each wave in the sequence may be separated from the next by between 15 and 60 minutes. The length of the waves depends on the depth of the ocean where they are travelling. At a typical ocean depth of four kilometres, the length of a tsunami wave is between 180 and 710 kilometres, and it travels at a speed of 200 metres per second, or 700 kilometres per hour.

The word tsunami is Japanese. Tsu means 'harbour', and nami means wave. The plural is the same as the singular (like the word 'sheep').

In shallow water near the coast, tsunami waves slow down and become shorter. When the sea is only 20 metres deep, their length decreases to between 13 and 50 kilometres, and their speed drops to 50 kilometres per hour. That's the good news. The bad news is that close to the coast tsunami start to increase in height. Measurements of tsunami waves in the deep ocean show that the wave height is usually less than half a metre. Given the right conditions, the same waves at the coast can reach heights of 30 to 35 metres.

Only a very few tsunami have produced larger waves. The largest tsunami measured along an open coast this century was 85 metres, recorded off Ishigaki, Japan in 1971. A wave that high would make even a big building like Te Papa pretty damp!

The EQC advertisement quoted above was therefore a little misleading. Tsunami waves are at their highest when they are travelling slowly in shallow water. They reach their top speed in deep water while they are still quite small.

The disturbances that produce tsunami are mainly associated with earthquakes; so tsunami are also called 'seismic sea waves'. The length of

Opposite: *A large tsunami was produced on 13 August 1868 by two major earthquakes (Richter magnitudes up to 8.5) that occurred four hours apart offshore from Arica in Chile. The initial tsunami was recognised by an 8-metre drop in water level. The subsequent wave was of the order of 20 metres high. It destroyed most of the ships in the harbour at Arica, and carried the USS Waterlee 400 metres inland. More than 25,000 people were killed along the Peru-Chile coast, and many coastal settlements, including Arica, were largely destroyed by the combined effects of the earthquakes and the tsunami.*

*This artist's impression of the largest tsunami wave approaching the USS Waterlee is the common perception of what a tsunami wave is like. However, most tsunami occur as a rapid rise and fall of water, not as a large breaking wave. If the wave had really been as depicted, the USS Waterlee would not have been carried on shore intact.*

(National Geographic Society)

'Great Wave off the Coast of Kanagawa', the classic woodcut by Hokusai, showing Mt Fuji with large waves tossing small fishing vessels in the foreground. Although this image is often used in tsunami publications, the waves depicted are wind-generated surf waves and not tsunami waves at all. Nonetheless, this is the way many people imagine that tsunami waves would appear to an observer on the beach.

tsunami waves is similar to the waves that produce the daily tides at the coast, so people often call them 'tidal waves'. This is a misnomer. True tidal waves are the result of the interaction between gravity and the rotation of the objects in the solar system, and the effect this interaction has on the Earth's surface. True tidal waves are even longer than tsunami (more than 2000 kilometres long, with wave crests more than three hours apart).

## Earthquakes and tsunami

Most tsunami waves that have been studied were caused by displacements on the ocean floor when earthquakes ruptured faults. Some of these tsunami were severe. The Lisbon Earthquake of 1 November

### Things that go bump

Tsunami waves are generated by large disturbances near the ocean floor. Different kinds of disturbance create different kinds of tsunami. The four main kinds are:

- displacements of the ocean floor caused by earthquakes
- mass flows travelling along the ocean floor
- explosions and collapses
- the impact of large objects falling into the ocean.

There are two other kinds of wave that are similar to tsunami:

- immediate waves or surges
- rissagas (also known as seebars, or meteorological tsunami).

1755 produced a tsunami with waves exceeding 10 metres in height that killed more than 50,000 people. The 1855 Wairarapa Earthquake in New Zealand produced a tsunami with waves of a similar height, but fortunately no casualties were recorded.

A tsunami is produced when the displacement of the ocean floor occurs along a considerable length of fault line. The tsunami source region is long and narrow, and produces a sequence of many waves that are stable and don't dissipate easily. The first waves are not the largest, and the wave period (the time between the wave tops) is reasonably long, between 15 and 30 minutes.

Because the tsunami waves are very stable, they can travel great distances, such as from one side of the Pacific Ocean to the other. We call these long-distance waves teletsunami. Over large distances the wave initially spreads out (like ripples in a pond), but eventually the curvature of the Earth starts to concentrate the wave again. At this point the tsunami increases in height and can become very destructive. It is because tsunami can cause great damage far from the source of the disturbance that they are so hazardous.

Typically, an earthquake that generates tsunami will have lifted up a chunk of the ocean floor. These are called dip-slip earthquakes. It takes a reasonably big earthquake to generate tsunami. Generally the

*Most tsunami damage occurs as a result of debris carried by the wave. This photo shows fishing vessels that were carried inland at Kodiak, Alaska, by the 28 March 1964 tsunami wave, and deposited amongst the remains of the wharf facilities. (United States Geological Survey)*

*This advertisement was one of a series produced during an EQC advertising campaign used in the late 1980s to highlight natural hazards and the need for individual disaster insurance. It is based on a common perception of tsunami hazard: a very large, fast breaking wave bearing down on the coast and sweeping all before it. However, this perception is unrealistic. (EQC)*

*These are well known images of waves produced by the 1 April 1946 Aleutian tsunami in Hilo Harbour, Hawaii. This harbour resonates in response to tsunami, producing very large breaking waves, as seen here. The largest wave destroyed the wharf at Hilo and killed the stevedore (arrowed). These photos were taken from the bridge of the SS Brigham Victory, which was carrying 50 tons of explosives and was attempting to sail out of the harbour. Although they were able to get out of the harbour, they were unable to escape from Hilo Bay against the force of the tsunami waves. This tsunami led to the establishment of the Pacific Tsunami Warning Centre. (NOAA)*

earthquake must be shallow (less than 70 kilometres) and have a magnitude of more than 7 on the Richter scale.

A few tsunami have been generated by shallow earthquakes with magnitudes as low as 5. These are unusual earthquakes known as tsunami earthquakes, and they cause larger displacements for their size than expected, perhaps because of landslides triggered by the earthquake, or because the earthquake's surface waves were amplified by soft marine sediments. New Zealand has experienced several tsunami earthquakes this century. Two occurred off Gisborne in 1947 and generated tsunami waves 5 to 10 metres high along the coast.

## Mass flows: making a splash!

Several different kinds of mass flows can create tsunami. They can be caused by landslides, by lahars and debris avalanches from volcanoes, by pyroclastic flows entering the ocean during volcanic eruptions, or by icebergs calving from glaciers. (There is more information in Chapter 2 about lahars and pyroclastic flows.)

Since mass flows are quite small and localised, compared to the large areas affected by earthquake displacements, their effect is more like dropping a large object into a swimming pool. A sequence of waves is produced, and the waves spread in concentric circles and dissipate quickly. The first wave is the biggest, but often the first two waves are similar in size, and the rest very small. Close to the source the waves may be very large, and unlike earthquake tsunami the waves may come close together (only 5 to 15 minutes apart).

Nonetheless, the tsunami produced by mass flows may be very large. Lituya Bay in Alaska is famous for producing the largest waves ever observed on Earth. (Four of the six eyewitnesses survived!) Lituya Bay is an estuary surrounded on three sides by mountains and glaciers, similar to the fiords in Fiordland. On 9 July 1958 an earthquake triggered a landslide containing 61 million cubic metres of rock, mud, and ice. When the landslide entered the water it produced an initial surge that rose an amazing 530 metres up the opposite side of the bay! Then the surge collapsed and produced a tsunami that was at least 60 metres high when it left the estuary.

*The 9 July 1958 tsunami in Lituya Bay was an extremely large event. It was produced by an enormous landslide that fell into a small confined bay. The resulting surge of water rose to 530 metres above sea level, and produced a 60-metre high tsunami at the entrance to the bay. This photo shows the impact of the tsunami on the forest at the entrance of Lituya Bay. A 600-metre swath of trees has been smashed into small fragments.*

*(NOAA)*

There is evidence that similar events at Lituya Bay produced tsunami waves of 61 metres in 1899, 120 metres in 1853, and 150 metres in 1936. In contrast, the biggest similar event in New Zealand, during the 1931 Napier Earthquake, produced only a 15-metre wave.

The largest tsunami waves (30 to 50 metres high) generated by the 1883 Krakatau Eruption were produced by 11 cubic kilometres of pyroclastic flows which poured into the

sea shortly before the volcano collapsed into a caldera. Some very large tsunami (365 metres high) were generated by submarine slumps and debris avalanches falling from steep lava flows rolling down the flanks of the Hawaiian volcanoes.

Although these tsunami can be very large close to the source, they grow smaller and vanish very quickly. There's no need for New Zealanders to worry about a tsunami 365 metres high that was created in Hawaii, because it will dissipate thousands of kilometres away.

*The Tatapouri Hotel near Gisborne was struck by two tsunami waves during the 25 March 1947 tsunami. These waves destroyed some small outbuildings between the hotel and the sea. The water level rose to the window sill level, and the receding water swept most of the furnishings out of the bar. This event is one of the largest local tsunami in New Zealand this century, and it is unusual in that it was produced by a small earthquake.*

*(Royal Society of New Zealand)*

## Explosion tsunami

Several different kinds of explosion can cause a depressed, crater-like region on the sea-bed, such as underwater explosions caused by submarine volcanoes, the collapse of the ocean floor during a volcanic eruption, nuclear explosions (and other non-natural underwater explosions), or explosions caused by the sudden release of natural gas. A very large amount of energy is required to produce a hazardous tsunami, because the process is not very efficient.

The initial disturbance forms tsunami waves as the water rebounds. The area affected is usually quite small compared with earthquake displacements, so the 'explosion' acts as a point source. Only a short sequence of tsunami waves is produced, and the largest wave is normally one of the first two waves, with the height decreasing rapidly with subsequent waves. The gap between the waves is quite short (less than 10 minutes). The largest tsunami due to submarine explosions have been only a few metres high at source.

Submarine volcanic activity can produce underwater explosions. The submarine Rumble volcanoes between New Zealand and the Kermadec Islands were detected by hydrophones that picked up the small explosions made by gases venting from their craters.

Collapse of the ocean floor to form a caldera during a volcanic eruption can also create tsunami. The 1883 Krakatau Eruption resulted in a caldera seven kilometres in diameter and several hundreds of metres deep. The caldera formed a hole that water rushed into, forming tsunami waves in the same way as an explosion crater. The tsunami created when the caldera formed were small, however (around five metres).

During the Cold War there was a lot of research done on the use of explosives to trigger tsunami waves. Alistair Maclean wrote a novel called *Goodbye California* which was based on the premise of nuclear bombs creating very large waves. Fortunately, research has shown that generating waves with explosives is extremely inefficient, and the resulting waves are small.

Gas hydrates are unstable mixtures of water and natural gas. Under pressure they form an icy matrix in ocean floor sediments that can collapse explosively to release gas, water, and mud. Explosions involving gas hydrates have been suggested as the cause of some large prehistoric tsunami in the North Sea. A very large explosion 55 million years ago is thought to have supercharged the Greenhouse Effect, warming the Earth and accelerating the evolution of mammals.

# Deep impact!

There is a constant rain of material falling to Earth from outer space (about 100,000 tonnes every year). Most of it is very small dust particles, but there are larger objects too. These meteorites (also known as bolides) are defined as weighing more than 1 kg. Between 100 and 300 of them fall every year. Larger objects may hit the Earth's surface with considerable energy. Depending on the mass of the meteorite, an impact in an ocean could produce tsunami waves with heights of several kilometres.

Since an impact is a point source, the waves would dissipate rapidly. However, numerical models indicate that stable tsunami waves with heights of 50 to 100 metres could be formed by meteorites as small as 200 metres in diameter. Objects of this size strike the Pacific Ocean with return periods of 24,000 to 43,000 years. This means that there is at least a 0.002 per cent chance of an impact occurring this year. To put the risk in perspective, the chance of winning first division Lotto is much less likely: only 0.000000036 per cent per game. In fact, the Lotto odds are very close to the probability of a bolide of 110 kilometres in diameter hitting Earth this year. There is good evidence to show that a meteorite impact near Yucatan 65 million years ago produced a tsunami that was at least 90 metres high along the coast of Texas. This event, along with volcanism-induced climate change, has been implicated in the extinction of the dinosaurs.

*The effect of the impact of a tsunami wave on a timber-framed school building during the 1992 Nicaragua tsunami. This photo demonstrates the tremendous force exerted by the tsunami, and also the amount of debris that can be transported by the waves. Most deaths due to tsunami are caused by injuries inflicted by floating debris.*
(NOAA)

## Immediate waves

An immediate wave is the surge produced directly by the displacement of the water during an earthquake, mass flow, explosion, or impact. If it continues to travel away from the source as a wave, it is called a tsunami.

However, the wave may just inundate the adjacent coast and not travel at all. This is often the case in confined areas such as harbours, where the shoreline is very steep or vertical (such as along wharves and sea walls). Immediate waves are very hazardous. In May 1983 a class of Japanese school children was killed by an immediate wave that struck while they were fishing from a wharf. The wave also lifted the boats tied up alongside the wharf and swept them ashore.

*This photo shows fishing vessels stranded on a wharf following the 26 May 1983 tsunami in the Sea of Japan. School children fishing nearby were swept away and drowned. (International Tsunami Information Centre and Japanese Meteorological Agency)*

## Rissagas

Rissagas are also known as seebar and meteorological tsunami. They are widely separated shallow water waves that behave as tsunami, though they are not generated by disturbances near the ocean floor, or even within the ocean. Instead they are generated by disturbances in the atmosphere through a process called 'phase coupling'. This occurs when the atmospheric disturbance travels at the same speed as a tsunami wave in the ocean, allowing energy to be transferred from the atmosphere to the ocean.

The 1883 Krakatau Eruption generated pressure waves that travelled around the Earth several times, and generated tsunami in many places far from the eruption. One was observed in the English Channel and another reached heights of 1.2 metres around the New Zealand coast. The Krakatau pressure waves also caused large lakes in New Zealand to seiche, that is, to slop from side to side (just as water in a container slops when it is tilted).

The large eruption from Lake Taupo 1800 years ago would have produced strong atmospheric pressure waves capable of generating tsunami. Tsunami deposits of the right age have been found around Cook Strait, and scientists hope to match them with historical accounts of tsunami from China, Japan, and the Mediterranean to provide an exact date for the Taupo eruption.

## Just how dangerous are tsunami?

A tsunami interacts with the coast to produce a variety of hazards, but the hazards created are specific to any section of coast. For example, the 1993 Hokkaido-Nansei-Oki tsunami varied in height from 5 to 30.5 metres along a short stretch of coast (half a kilometre in length) on Okushiri Island, Japan, with the damage it caused varying in different places. It is very difficult to generalise about the kinds of hazards created, because tsunami are very rarely generated from exactly the same source in the same way, so they behave differently as they travel.

The potential tsunami hazard is normally evaluated by something called the 'maximum tsunami wave run-up'. The run-up can be measured as either the vertical height that the wave reaches, or the horizontal distance the wave floods inland (the extent of the inundation). Because the inundation distance depends on how high the wave is at the shore as well as the local topography, the vertical run-up is a more reliable indicator.

Above: *The 12 July 1993 Hokkaido-Nansei-Oki tsunami varied in height from 10-30 metres around the coast of Okushiri Island, and up to 10 metres on the coast of Hokkaido where this photo was taken. Along the Hokkaido coast 200 homes were destroyed, contributing to the debris shown. This region was also affected by the 26 May 1983 tsunami. Memories of this earlier event contributed to the rapid evacuation of the coastal area, leading to a limited death toll of 120 in the 1993 event.*
(University of Tokyo)

Left: *The 12 July 1993 Hokkaido-Nansei-Oki tsunami sunk or swept away nearly 270 small vessels along the coast. Those that were swept inland contributed to the damage, either through impact or by fire.*
(University of Tokyo)

*These photos show the railway bridge at Wailuku River, Hilo Bay. During the 1 April 1946 Aleutian tsunami, bores formed and severely damaged the bridge, removing one of the spans. (NOAA)*

## Tsunami bores

The most destructive tsunami are those that form a bore. This may seem strange, since a breaking wave is losing energy and would therefore have less energy at the shore than a wave of the same size that does not break. The damage is mainly caused by the turbulence in the wave.

Tsunami bores can lift and carry quite large objects. For example, bores associated with the 1960 Chilean tsunami transported 20 tonne pieces of a Japanese sea wall as far as 200 metres inland!

Tsunami bores in estuaries and the lower reaches of rivers and streams are the most common features of tsunami in New Zealand, and have caused most of the severe damage. It used to be common practice to build road and rail bridges at the upper limit of tidal influence on coastal rivers and streams. This provided some protection from floods coming down the channel. Unfortunately this is also the position where the tsunami bores are strongest. Quite a few coastal bridges and their approaches have been damaged or destroyed by tsunami in New Zealand. For example, one of the 1947 Gisborne tsunami formed a bore that carried the main beams and deck of the Pouawa River Bridge 1.5 kilometres upriver.

*Tsunami bores have caused most of the recorded tsunami damage in New Zealand. They are particularly effective at the upper limit of the tide in rivers and estuaries, which happens to be where many bridges are built. This photo shows the site of the bridge across the Pouawa River north of Gisborne following the 25 March 1947 tsunami. (Royal Society of New Zealand)*

## Floating debris

Floating debris is another tsunami hazard. During the 1993 Hokkaido-Nansei-Oki tsunami most deaths and injuries were due to the impact of floating debris. It has been found that floating wood pushed by tsunami bores may exert impulsive forces of more than 9 tonnes – more than many structures can withstand.

Tsunami may also spread liquid contaminants such as oil. In ports there are many sources of fuel oils, diesel, and lighter hydrocarbons, all of which can burn. Many refuelling facilities in New Zealand ports and marinas do not protect fuel-supply pipes from the effects of tsunami. Combustible materials carried by tsunami may also be ignited by sparks from electrical equipment as they are inundated by tsunami waves. The 1960 Chilean tsunami caused several electrical failures at Lyttelton, though no major fires resulted.

The most hazardous floating debris appears to be small boats in marinas or fishing ports. In Japan small fishing vessels swept inland by tsunami waves have been a major cause of fires associated with tsunami.

*This photo shows the aftermath 12 July 1993 Hokkaido-Nansei-Oki tsunami. The large amount of floating debris (including a wrecked boat) carried by the tsunami waves is clearly evident. Debris greatly adds to the destructive power of the tsunami.*

(University of Tokyo)

### To break or not to break

When tsunami travel across the continental shelf they may break down into a series of separate waves, just as swell waves break down in the surf zone at the beach. The separate waves produced by tsunami can behave in two ways:

- a non-breaking wave that behaves like a rapidly rising and falling tide. In this case the maximum run-up is equal to the height of the wave when it reaches dry land (although it can be higher if the coast is very steep).

- a breaking wave (also known as a bore). This is the type of wave many people believe to be typical of tsunami (perhaps because of the EQC advertisement). The maximum run-up is less than the height of the bore when it reaches dry land.

Most tsunami reaching the New Zealand coast have behaved as non-breaking waves, although they have tended to form breaking waves in estuaries.

### Return flow

The currents generated by the receding tsunami wave can be high. The 1998 Saundaun tsunami in Papua New Guinea generated flow velocities of 10-20 metres per second. Most drownings associated with tsunami have been when people are swept into deep water by the wave on its return journey out to sea. The return flow may also carry floating debris with the same potential for injury and damage as an advancing tsunami bore.

## What happens in harbours, estuaries, and rivers?

Tsunami waves may force oscillations within semi-enclosed basins such as estuaries, harbours, and the lower reaches of rivers to produce a seiche. Wellington Harbour resonates in response to tsunami, which has the effect of increasing the height of the tsunami, particularly in Evans Bay.

A tsunami may cause rapid changes in water level in an estuary. Even if the change in level is small it will generate strong currents. Most historical tsunami in New Zealand have produced strong currents and eddies in estuaries around the coast. These currents have caused much of the damage in harbours. Vessels break their moorings because of rapid changes in the strength and direction of the tsunami currents. Harbour channels can change position due to the scouring and re-deposition of sediments on the sea floor. The 1868 Chilean tsunami, for example, completely realigned the main channel into Otago Harbour, requiring a new survey by the Harbour Pilot before it could be used

*In Japan, sea walls have been constructed to provide protection from tsunami waves. This has been found to be an expensive and somewhat ineffectual approach. They do offer some protection from small tsunami, but do not work for large waves, and the materials used to construct the sea wall often contribute to the damage caused.*

(University of Tokyo)

by shipping. The 1960 Chilean tsunami caused severe erosion around the entrances to several estuaries along the east coast of the North Island, at Napier, Ohiwa Harbour, and Maketu.

## Can anything be done about tsunami?

Tsunami are a serious hazard, particularly around the Pacific Ocean, in the Caribbean, and around the Mediterranean. There are two main approaches to reducing the risk: protective measures, such as barriers, effective building design, or planning restrictions; and evacuation procedures. The effectiveness of all these things is continually monitored by international agencies, such as the International Tsunami Commission.

Protective structures are used in areas that are subject to frequent tsunami inundation, or that contain essential infrastructure.

Coastal barriers such as sea walls and tidal barrages across river mouths have been found to be very expensive, and may adversely affect the environment. In order to be effective, the expected tsunami height must be accurately predicted. Japan is the leading user of coastal barriers. Recent tsunami have demonstrated that their structures are ineffective. This is mainly because the locals assumed that the barriers would give them complete protection, but the tsunami were bigger than expected and over-topped and destroyed the structures.

Tsunami forests are coastal tree plantations which increase the flow resistance of coastal land. The forests absorb the tsunami energy, reducing the distance they travel inland. This approach is becoming increasingly popular with Pacific Rim countries such as Japan, Korea, the Philippines, and Indonesia. However, bear in mind that the tsunami forests are intended to *slow down* the tsunami waves and may not stop them. During the Saundaun Tsunami of 17 July 1998, thickets of *Casuarina* trees greatly reduced the inundation by the tsunami, whereas the coconut palms snapped off at ground level and increased the tsunami's impact. The International Tsunami Survey Team recommended that the villages be relocated behind rows of *Casuarina* to reduce the impact of future tsunami.

Tsunami-resistant buildings can be used where it is not feasible to install coastal protection. The lowest floors are designed to cope with the occasional tsunami inundation, often using an open structure for car-parking while fully enclosing the engineering plant within reinforced structures that can withstand the very high tsunami forces. Te Papa has been designed to be tsunami-resistant.

Planning restrictions can also be used to limit development in areas subject to tsunami inundation. For example, in 1946 a tsunami struck Hilo in Hawaii and caused extensive damage to the central business district. The city planners decided to prevent the reconstruction of the damaged buildings between the main street and the sea, and created a tsunami reserve that became a park with large car parks. Unfortunately the next large tsunami in 1960 flowed unimpeded across the tsunami reserve and inflicted severe damage further inland.

For protective structures and planning measures to be effective, the likely tsunami hazard must be able to be well defined. In many places this is not possible, which means that good evacuation procedures provide the best protection.

## Evacuation procedures

Tsunami specialists agree that the most effective way of mitigating the tsunami hazard is to evacuate affected areas promptly. To do this you must have an effective warning system and be able to respond quickly to a warning. The warning system must be able to correctly identify all approaching tsunami, with no false alarms. People respond rapidly in regions where tsunami occur frequently (that is, less than 30 years apart). It is usually hard to evacuate people when tsunami are an infrequent hazard (as in New Zealand). Public education programmes can improve people's response rates, but experiencing a tsunami is the most effective education anyone can have.

The priority for most countries, therefore, is the development of an effective warning system. Most countries which experience tsunami have a national organisation to handle tsunami warnings. There are usually two systems: an

*Below left and right: Tsunami waves are very erosive and can greatly alter the coast. These photos show some of the erosion caused by a tsunami in Indonesia. The land was eroded for 100 metres inland by a series of waves.* (NOAA)

international warning system, such as the Pacific Tsunami Warning Center (PTWC); and local warning systems, such as that operated by the Japan Meteorological Agency (JMA).

The PTWC was developed following a tsunami in 1946 that caused severe damage in Hawaii, and expanded rapidly after the 1960 Chilean tsunami struck. The system is very effective for

*Above: Following the 1 April 1946 tsunami, the authorities in Hilo, Hawaii decided to convert the area damaged by the tsunami into a car park to prevent a repeat of the destruction. The first of these photos shows the car park prior to the 22 May 1960 Chilean tsunami. Unfortunately this tsunami swept straight across the open space and destroyed the buildings that had been unaffected in 1946. The force of the water is demonstrated by the effect it had on the parking meters in the car park.*
*(NOAA)*

dealing with teletsunami warnings.

A network of seismometers is linked to a central processing facility. When large earthquakes occur, their epicentre, focal depth and magnitude are calculated. (At present this takes 15 minutes.) If the earthquake is considered capable of generating a tsunami, the PTWC notifies the national organisations in countries likely to be affected. This is done as a Tsunami Watch Bulletin, which advises that a major earthquake has occurred and that a tsunami is probable.

## Great tsunami of the past

New Zealand has experienced at least 33 historic and prehistoric tsunami (see box). There are two main kinds. Teletsunami, which have been generated beyond the New Zealand continental shelf, have longer periods and persist for several days. They affect most of the New Zealand coast.

In contrast, local tsunami which have been generated on the New Zealand continental shelf have shorter periods, do not last long, and only affect a part of the New Zealand coast.

*The approach of the 26 May 1983 tsunami along the Japanese coast. These images show the presence of a turbulent crest (the light zones), but the waves are not the vertical wall of water evident in the artist's impression of the 1868 Chilean tsunami. (Japanese Meteorological Agency)*

### Warning!

The PTWC collects tide-gauge data from the regions surrounding the earthquake, looking for evidence of a tsunami, and runs computer simulations to determine the likely travel times and wave heights given the earthquake location and size. These are continually updated and the results passed on to the countries likely to be affected. Depending on the information obtained after the earthquake, the PTWC can issue two types of bulletins:

- Tsunami Information Bulletin – no tsunami has been generated and no further action is required

- Tsunami Warning Bulletin – a tsunami has been generated and may affect all or part of the Pacific.

The national organisations evaluate the information and determine which areas will be affected and require evacuation. This system works well for areas that are sufficiently far from the source to allow for the delays, but it is less effective for local tsunami.

The JMA maintains a local warning system for Japan. This presently involves 180 seismic stations and 77 tide gauges linked to a central facility. The JMA can determine the location and characteristics of an earthquake within three minutes of the first motion. Their aim is to issue the necessary warnings to local authorities within five minutes of an event. For most local tsunami this provides sufficient time to evacuate coastal areas if the people respond quickly.

# Tsunami that have struck New Zealand

| Date | Source | Max. NZ run-up (metres) | Comments |
| --- | --- | --- | --- |
| 1800 BP | Lake Taupo | unknown | Rissaga caused by eruption |
| AD 350 | Cook Strait | unknown | Local earthquake |
| AD 1220 | Cook Strait | unknown | Local earthquake |
| AD 1440 | Cook Strait | unknown | Local earthquake |
| c. 1820 | Probably Foveaux Strait | >10 m ? | Many killed at Orepuki |
| 15 Oct. 1848 | Lower Wairau Valley | 0.3 | |
| 23 Jan. 1855 | West Wairarapa | 9.1 | |
| March 1856 | Chatham Rise | | Uncertain event |
| 13 Aug. 1868 | Chile | 3.1 | |
| 10 May 1877 | Chile | 3.7 | |
| 27 Aug. 1883 | Krakatau, Indonesia | 1.8 | Rissaga caused by eruption |
| 22 June 1891 | Waikato Heads | | Uncertain event |
| 22 Feb. 1913 | Westport | 1.5 | Landslide |
| 1 May 1917 | Kermadec Islands | ? | Recorded in California |
| 11 Nov. 1922 | Chile | 0.2 | |
| 25 Dec. 1922 | Rangiora | 0.4 | Probably an immediate wave |
| 1 Sep. 1923 | Kwanto, Japan | <0.1 | |
| 1927-1928 | Tolaga Bay | >4 | 3 large waves |
| 16 June 1929 | Whitecliffs, Karamea | 2.5 | Landslide |
| 2 Feb. 1931 | Waikare, Hawke Bay | 15.3 | Landslide |
| 2 Feb. 1931 | Napier | ~3 | |
| 25 Mar. 1947 | Gisborne | 10.0 | 2 large waves |
| 17 May 1947 | Gisborne | 6.0 | |
| 14 Mar 1950 | Bay of Plenty | | Uncertain event |
| 4 Nov. 1952 | Kamchatka | 0.9 | |
| 22 May 1960 | Chile | 3.5 | Largest tsunami this century |
| 28 Mar. 1964 | Alaska | 0.9 | |
| 14 Jan. 1976 | Kermadec Islands | 0.8 | |
| 22 June 1977 | Tonga | <0.2 | |
| 25 May 1981 | Macquarie Ridge | 0.3 | |
| Dec. 1982 | Kermadec Islands | <0.1 | |
| Oct.1986 | Kermadec Islands | <0.1 | |
| 20 May 1987 | Doubtful Sound | 3.0 | Landslide |
| June 1993 | Kermadec Islands | <0.1 | |
| 6 Oct. 1994 | Kuril Islands | <0.1 | |
| 16 Jan. 1995 | Japan | 0.1 | Kobe Earthquake |
| 25 Mar.1998 | Balleny Islands | 0.2 | |
| 17 July 1998 | Sissano Lagoon, PNG | 0.3 | |

This photo shows the crest of the 9 March 1957 Aleutian tsunami reaching the shore at Oahu, Hawaii. The wave is behaving as a rapidly rising tide, and is flowing around the house on the foredune of the beach. The flow velocities are 1-3 metres per second, which is too fast to swim against. This is the typical type of behaviour exhibited by tsunami in New Zealand.

(NOAA)

## Teletsunami

Most historic teletsunami have been quite small (smaller than half a metre) and have had minimal impact on the New Zealand coast. However, a few have been large enough to cause extensive damage. The last of these occurred before the extensive coastal developments that started in the 1970s. A large teletsunami these days would do much more damage than those in the past.

Using computer models and historical data, we can assess which earthquakes around the Pacific Rim are likely to produce teletsunami that could cause damage on the New Zealand coast. The National Geophysical Data Center of the National Oceanic and Atmospheric Administration (NOAA) in Boulder, Colorado has defined 10 tsunami-generating regions for the Pacific region, covering Hawaii, New Guinea and the Solomon Islands, Japan, the Aleutian Islands and Alaska, South America and so on.

We can ignore some regions as potential generators of significant teletsunami affecting New Zealand. Hawaii, Papua New Guinea, the Solomon Islands, Indonesia, and the Philippines can all be ruled out, either because they are unlikely to generate teletsunami or because the route they would have to travel here is indirect, and a tsunami would dissipate before it arrived.

Next we have the regions that represent a minimal hazard. These are the islands of the South Pacific, Japan and the Kuril Islands, and Kamchatka. They have all generated teletsunami recorded in New Zealand in the past. However, the travel paths of the Northwest Pacific tsunami involve considerable energy dissipation so the resulting tsunami are small, with waves less than half a metre high. The Southwest Pacific tsunami are generated by tectonic structures that direct the tsunami waves away from New Zealand, so the resulting waves are also small in New Zealand. Shallow earthquakes greater than magnitude 7.5 near the Kermadec Islands can generate waves of up to 75 centimetres in northern New Zealand. For sources further north, it takes a much larger earthquake to create a detectable wave.

The 13 August 1868 Chilean tsunami was first noticed when there was an 8-metre drop in water level in the harbour at Arica, Chile. This is an artist's impression of the recession which left the USS Waterlee and other vessels stranded. Often recession is taken to be the first sign of an approaching tsunami. However, the initial movement of the water depends on how the tsunami was generated. An upward displacement of the sea-floor produces an upwards initial movement. Most tsunami events start with an upward movement, but it may be small and go unnoticed until the following wave trough arrives. Tsunami recession has been a significant feature of some tsunami events in New Zealand, such as the 2 February 1931 Napier tsunami at Mahia Peninsula, and the 22 May 1960 Chilean tsunami at Whitianga.
(National Geographic Society)

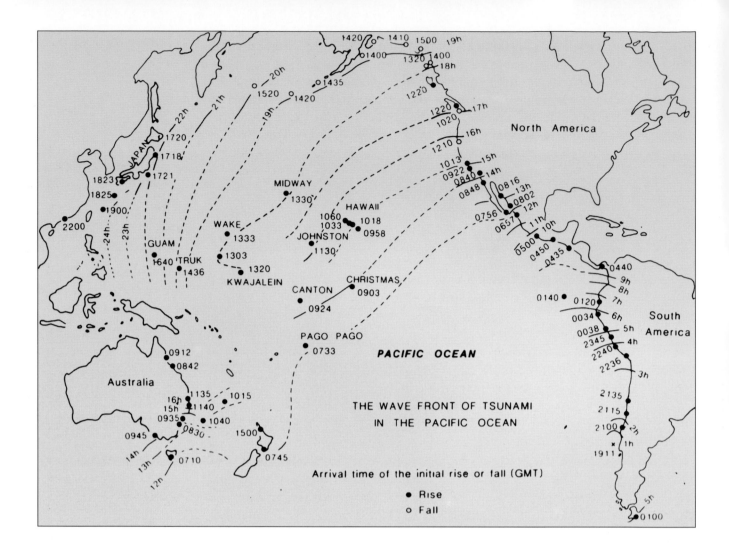

THE WAVE FRONT OF TSUNAMI
IN THE PACIFIC OCEAN

PACIFIC OCEAN

Arrival time of the initial rise or fall (GMT)

● Rise
○ Fall

*This map shows the travel times of the 1960 Chilean tsunami. Although the tsunami travels quickly, it still takes 12-14 hours for most teletsunami to reach the New Zealand region. This provides sufficient time for Civil Defence to initiate the necessary procedures to deal with the tsunami. The map also shows the way the tsunami is distorted by the variations in water depth in the Pacific Ocean: the wave is slower in shallow water.*

*(NOAA)*

Based on historical data, a significant teletsunami in New Zealand must have been generated by a very shallow earthquake, bigger than Richter magnitude 8.25, located on the east coast of Kamchatka, Japan, or the Kuril Islands.

The Aleutian Islands and Alaska are a moderate hazard. Only one historic teletsunami has been recorded from this region, on 28 March 1964. This event produced wave heights up to 1.5 metres around the New Zealand coast. It seems likely that only very shallow earthquakes with Richter magnitudes of 8 and above will produce a significant tsunami in New Zealand.

The West Coast of South America represents the greatest hazard. Four teletsunami have been recorded in New Zealand, and three of the most destructive events (in 1868, 1877, and 1960) came from this region. All the historical teletsunami have been associated with shallow earthquakes with Richter magnitudes greater than 8.2, and have produced wave heights up to 5 metres. Numerical modelling

suggests that magnitudes as low as 7.6 may produce a significant wave in New Zealand.

This leaves one region of uncertainty: the west coast of North and Central America. No historic teletsunami have been recorded from this region. Numerical modelling suggests that the tectonic structures in Central America may direct tsunami towards the Northwest Pacific, so that New Zealand would not be affected. However, further north, tsunami may be directed towards the Southwest Pacific. Research in Oregon suggests that tsunami are generated in this region by very large earthquakes. It is likely that the west coast of North America represents a moderate to high teletsunami hazard for New Zealand.

## Where do tsunami strike?

Some parts of New Zealand's coast are more vulnerable to tsunami than others. The east coast is more susceptible than the west coast, because most tsunami come from the east of New Zealand, while tsunami coming from the west or north-west are blocked by islands and shallow seas. Tsunami waves from the eastern Pacific Ocean do reach the west coast of New Zealand, mostly by reflecting off the Great Barrier Reef of Australia, but they are smaller and arrive a lot later than the direct waves reaching the east coast of New Zealand.

The effect of tsunami along the east coast varies from location to location. The danger regions are Banks Peninsula and Poverty Bay. For Banks Peninsula, resonance in Pegasus Bay appears to amplify the waves, though it's also possible the Chatham Rise may concentrate tsunami energy on the Peninsula. Numerical modelling of the 1960 Chilean tsunami demonstrated that similar ridges off Japan could increase tsunami wave heights by 200-300 per cent. Similar increases were observed around Banks Peninsula during the 1868, 1877, and 1960 Chilean tsunami.

Numerical modelling of Poverty Bay shows that resonance occurs here too, amplifying the tsunami waves.

There are also more localised areas where refraction of tsunami waves around offshore islands concentrates the wave energy, producing larger tsunami (such as Omaha Bay); where funnel-shaped embayments concentrate the tsunami energy at the head of the bay (as in Mercury Bay); or where the tsunami causes estuaries to seiche, which amplifies the waves (as in Wellington Harbour).

The main regions where tsunami are smaller than average are Cook Strait and the north of the South Island, and the Firth of Thames. Teletsunami recorded within Cook

Below, from left to right: *One of the human facets of tsunami mitigation is the need to overcome curiosity. There were two main responses to the 1960 Chilean tsunami from the various coastal populations in New Zealand that were affected. One was a panicked flight to the nearest safe high ground. The other response was to head down to the coast to watch the tsunami waves. Here a large group of Gisborne residents has assembled at the waterfront to observe the tsunami.* (Gisborne District Council)
*The maximum height of the tsunami wave on the wharf hut shown in the first photo. The tsunami here is behaving like a 6-metre rapidly rising and falling tide. Earlier (at night) the tsunami generated a 1.2-metre bore on the nearby Waimata and Taruheru Rivers that caused some damage.* (Gisborne District Council)
*A flattened fence at Turihaua Point following the 25 March 1947 tsunami. This illustrates the force exerted by the tsunami wave: large-diameter strainer posts were snapped off at ground level. Seaweed was also found here in the overhead telephone wires, indicating a wave height of at least 10 metres.* (Courtesy of the Gisborne Museum and Arts Centre)

Strait, the Marlborough Sounds, Tasman Bay, and Golden Bay tend to be smaller than those nearby on the east coast. The shallow waters of the Inner Hauraki Gulf dissipate the tsunami energy, producing smaller waves in the Firth of Thames.

*Outbuildings of the Tatapouri
Hotel after the 25 March 1947
tsunami.*
(Royal Society of New
Zealand)

*These fish were collected from
inside the Tatapouri Hotel
following the 25 March 1947
tsunami.*
(Courtesy of the Gisborne
Museum and Arts Centre)

## Local tsunami

Local tsunami are caused by a variety of mechanisms including earthquakes, landslides, and volcanic eruptions, and include the largest tsunami recorded in New Zealand. They can be generated anywhere around the New Zealand coast, though three regions are more likely to generate local tsunami: the East Coast from Poverty Bay to East Cape, Cook Strait, and the West Coast.

The continental shelf off Poverty Bay and East Cape seems to produce a large number of tsunami earthquakes and the tsunami are much larger than you would expect from the size of the earthquake. It appears that the tsunami are being produced by mud volcanoes along the offshore Ariel Bank. Several large mud eruptions were recorded this century about 20 kilometres north of Gisborne in the Mangaehu and Waimata Valleys. The first was on 25 July 1908, and produced an eruption column about 120 metres high, depositing some 150,000 cubic metres of material around the vent. Another occurred on 6 May 1930, and deposited 270,000 cubic metres of material. Neither eruption was accompanied by seismic activity. At the coast, 100,000 square metres of sea floor in Sponge Bay, near Gisborne, rose two metres within a few minutes on 17 February 1931. Once again, no seismic activity was observed.

Numerical modelling also has shown that mud eruptions are the most likely cause of the large tsunami of 25 March and 17 May 1947 that struck the coast between Mahia Peninsula and Tolaga Bay. The same mechanism probably also generated the tsunami waves that damaged Tolaga Bay wharf while it was being built in 1927-8.

These tsunami are particularly hazardous because the earthquakes that cause them are small (and sometimes there is no earthquake), but the waves are quite large, between five and ten metres high. The travel time from the source to the coast is short, so there is very little warning of their arrival, and their impact is severe. Because local tsunami are relatively rare in New Zealand we have no warning system.

Several large fault zones associated with the Alpine Fault run across Cook Strait. One of these, the Wairarapa Fault, ruptured during the 1855 Wairarapa Earthquake, and created the largest earthquake-generated tsunami since 1840. Movement on the Awatere Fault may also have generated a tsunami seven years earlier, in 1848.

It is possible to identify prehistoric tsunami from the deposits they have left behind. Core samples taken from wetlands along the Cook Strait coast show that there have been at least five tsunami bigger than 10 metres during the last 2,000 years. (Because the large 1855 tsunami doesn't show up well in the sediment record, this suggests that the prehistoric tsunami may have been even larger than the deposits would indicate.) All of them seem to be associated with local earthquakes or with the Taupo eruption 1800 years ago.

Since we do not have much data on prehistoric events, it is hard to determine whether the tsunami hazard is greater than the earthquake hazard for coastal areas. But we do know that tsunami will make the impact of an earthquake in Cook Strait more severe. Nonetheless, tsunami in Cook Strait seem not to happen very often, so it is hard to justify the expense of building protective structures.

Although the west coast of New Zealand has been largely unaffected by historic tsunami, the West Coast and Fiordland have experienced several local tsunami generated by landslides. Landslide tsunami can be very large, particularly in confined waters such as the fiords. However, due to the sparse population in these areas, the human risk associated with local tsunami is low.

## Volcanic tsunami

No volcanic tsunami have been observed in New Zealand – so far. But because New Zealand straddles two tectonic plates, and has a good deal of volcanic activity, volcanic tsunami are always a possibility.

There are four main areas capable of generating a volcanic tsunami. The Auckland Volcanic Field consists of 48 basaltic volcanoes. In themselves, basaltic volcanoes are not a likely source of tsunami. However, numerical modelling shows that, given a vent in just the right place, a sequence of closely-spaced explosions could cause one to two-metre tsunami waves along the eastern beaches of Auckland (though they are more likely to be less than half a metre).

There are several offshore volcanic vents in the Bay of Plenty associated with the Taupo Volcanic Zone, particularly White Island and Mayor Island. Public concern over tsunami produced by an eruption of White Island (triggered by sea water entering the crater) led to the first numerical modelling of tsunami in New Zealand. Two independent studies have concluded that White Island would not generate large tsunami affecting the coast because it is in deep water beyond the continental shelf, and most of the energy that a tsunami produced would be reflected away from the coast. White Island is also unlikely to produce pyroclastic flows. But Mayor Island is on the continental shelf and has had several episodes of major eruptions producing pyroclastic flows. Numerical modelling shows that the largest credible eruptions at Mayor Island could produce 20-metre high tsunami along the Bay of Plenty coast.

The remaining volcanoes of the Taupo Volcanic Zone are on land, so you may think that they are incapable of generating tsunami. However, some of the volcanic centres are capable of producing very large eruptions (particularly Okataina and Lake Taupo), and at least two previous eruptions have generated tsunami.

The Rotoiti Eruption from the Okataina volcanic centre produced large pyroclastic flows that reached the sea in the Bay of Plenty. Some of these flows now form the sea cliffs near Matata. The flows caused large steam explosions that formed the Rotoehu Ash, and would have also generated tsunami. Numerical modelling indicates that these tsunami could have been up to 100 metres high at source. However they would have dissipated rapidly, reducing to less than 30 metres high near Tauranga.

The Taupo Eruption 1800 years ago also created large pyroclastic flows. The column collapse that produced the flows probably also generated large pressure waves in the atmosphere that formed rissaga around New Zealand. Since the Taupo eruption was bigger than the 1883 Krakatau Eruption, rissaga were probably generated world-wide. The rissaga around New Zealand were probably between two and five metres high.

## Tsunami alert!

Although we don't know a lot about tsunami affecting New Zealand, we can assess what size of tsunami can be expected in various places on the eastern coast of both islands. The indications are that Banks Peninsula and Poverty Bay are the most hazardous places as far as tsunami are concerned. And if you take into account the new data on prehistoric tsunami in Cook Strait, Wellington should probably be added to the list.

The Ministry of Civil Defence and Regional Councils are responsible for the mitigation of natural hazards in New Zealand. For teletsunami events the Ministry

Opposite: *Okataina volcanic centre is another potential tsunami generator. The picture shows Mount Tarawera in the centre, with Mount Edgecumbe behind and Lake Rotomahana in front. Okataina may generate tsunami when very large pyroclastic flows are produced and reach the sea, as has occurred several times in the past near Matata. Although the tsunami produced could be very large, most local inhabitants would probably be killed by the pyroclastic flows before the tsunami formed.*
(IGNS)

of Civil Defence receives all tsunami bulletins issued by the Pacific Tsunami Warning Centre.

When a Tsunami Watch Bulletin is received, the information is sent to Regional Councils and territorial authorities, the Police, the New Zealand Defence Force, and other organisations concerned with hazard mitigation. The public is not alerted unless the tsunami arrival time is estimated to be less than four hours (that is, only when the tsunami was generated within 3,000 kilometres of the coast).

A Tsunami Warning Bulletin indicates that a tsunami has been generated. If the arrival time is greater than four hours, the Ministry of Civil Defence consults its scientific advisers to determine how to respond. Depending on the level of the threat, the Ministry may issue tsunami warning bulletins to affected regions and the necessary authorities. The Ministry will also advise the public of the hazard. If the travel time is less than four hours, the Ministry will issue tsunami warning bulletins without waiting for scientific advice. The Regional Councils and territorial authorities have responsibility for evacuation procedures.

# Wet 'n wild

JIM SALINGER

New Zealand is a long, narrow, mountainous land, set in the watery Southern Hemisphere far to the east of the continent of Australia. Its high mountains and maritime setting make it particularly vulnerable to climatic hazards. Snow and drought, hail, high winds, and heavy rain all happen in New Zealand, and they can be much more severe than the rain, wind, snow, or droughts of the mid-latitude climates of countries in western Europe.

Severe storms or drought can wreak havoc on New Zealand's communities and its landscape. Climatic events such as these have shaped the land over millions of years. But these visitations of climatic hazards to our shores are not constant. The kind of weather we think of as being typically New Zealand weather has been vastly different at different times in the past, because of climate variability and change. The climate in the recent past was quite different from today's. For example, the first European explorers to climb the South Island mountains in the 1860s were confronted with a landscape with much more snow and ice than we see on the Southern Alps today. In winter, the landscape was cloaked in a snowy mantle of 100 cubic kilometres in volume. By the 1990s this had shrunk to 67 cubic kilometres of snow and ice. In contrast, two features of today's climate, El Niño and La Niña, that we think of as recent phenomena, have been regular visitors to New Zealand for hundreds of years, modifying and modulating the beat of our variable climate.

## What are climate hazards?

Every New Zealander has experienced one of the most notable climate hazards, heavy rainfall. Climate scientists define heavy rainfall as more than 100 millimetres of rain falling in a day (or a pro rata amount). One hundred millimetres of rain is about the depth of your hand, so 'heavy rain' is a deluge of a depth of your hand over a day, or a proportional amount falling over a smaller period of time. Heavy rainfall causes floods and landslides which may damage people's property, put their lives at risk, and damage the natural environment. In any one year, there are many heavy falls of rain in various parts of New Zealand.

In contrast, drought is sneaky. Unlike the other climate hazards, it tends to creep up on us unobtrusively until suddenly a disaster is upon us. When it rains, water tops up the soil for plant growth, and fills up our water-supply reservoirs and hydro lakes. As time passes (and if no more rain falls) plants push moisture out from the soil to the air, people use the water in the reservoirs, farmers use the water on their land for their animals or to irrigate their crops, and water from the hydro lakes is used to generate electricity. Eventually, if there is no rain to replenish

Opposite: *The destructive power of the weather!*
(Gisborne District Council)

## So what causes the weather?

The air on Planet Earth is a giant weather machine. It shunts the heat and energy coming from the sun around the planet. The equatorial regions receive too much heat and energy while the polar regions get too little. This imbalance of energy and heat between the equator and the poles creates our global weather. Like any engine, the weather machine has many parts. The weather machine creates the typical climate zones in the Northern and Southern Hemisphere. Moving out from the equator to the poles, these zones are:

- the Hadley Cell and intertropical convergence zone
- the subtropical anticyclonic belt
- the mid-latitude westerlies
- the low pressure belt circling the poles.

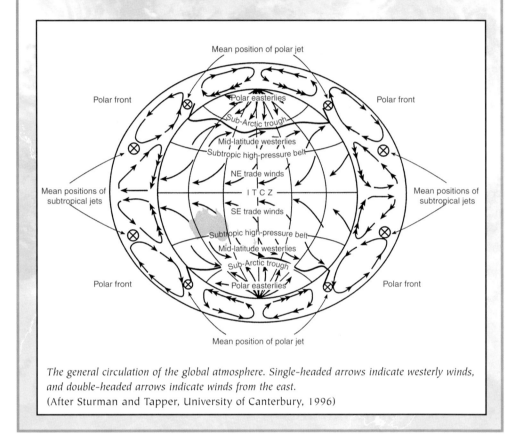

The general circulation of the global atmosphere. Single-headed arrows indicate westerly winds, and double-headed arrows indicate winds from the east.
(After Sturman and Tapper, University of Canterbury, 1996)

the water that is being used, the lakes and reservoirs run dry. It's as simple as balancing your spending against your income in your cheque book. Drought occurs when there is not enough water falling as rain to fulfil our requirements for farming, city dwelling, electricity generation, and so on. Although droughts in New Zealand are not as frequent as heavy rainfall, they have a huge impact.

A heavy fall of snow can disrupt all types of communications, cut power and all forms of transport, and kill large numbers of livestock. In New Zealand, heavy snowfall is said to occur when more than 25 centimetres of snow falls in a day, or 10 centimetres of snow falls in 6 hours. Heavy snowfalls occur frequently in our high country, but the more important events are those snowfalls in the lower hill country and near sea-level, because they have the most dramatic consequences: farm animals killed, roads blocked, telephone and power lines down.

A hailstorm is termed 'severe' when the hailstones are the size of peas, or cause damage to crops and other property. On average there are only about nine such

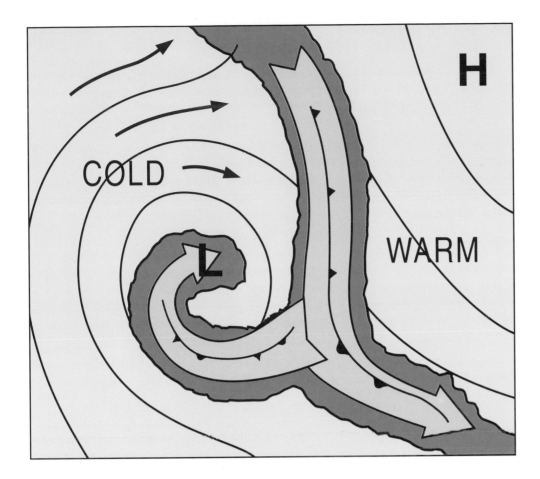

storms in any one year, and the area affected is small, so their effect on the community is much less than that of the other climate hazards. Hailstorms are usually not life threatening.

The last of the major climatic hazards is high wind. Windstorms can batter many areas of New Zealand. These may have very severe consequences, including loss of life, devastation to forests, and destruction of buildings. Southern New Zealand is on the edge of the Roaring Forties (the zone of strong westerly winds that occur between 40°South and 50°South), so we are especially prone to windstorms.

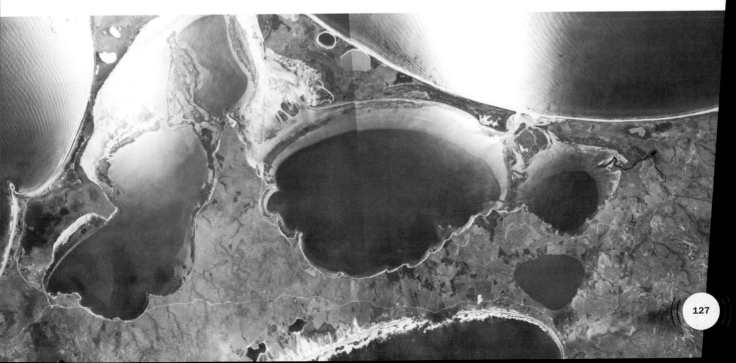

# Prevailing westerlies

New Zealand lies in the subtropical belt of anticyclones and mid-latitude westerlies. The belt of anticyclones causes very sunny dry climates in the latitudes they occupy because the anticyclones bring sinking dry air. This is in dramatic contrast to the busy zone of westerlies that lies further south. The depressions (also called lows) brought by the westerlies have a clockwise spin, and they vigorously mix the milder air from the north and north-west with cold subantarctic air from the south and south-west. The mixing of this cold air from the south with the milder moist air from further north sets off our depressions in the westerlies, bringing strong winds, rain, and snow.

New Zealand is located in the Southwest Pacific, a very special part of the global weather machine, in which a tug of war is going on all the time between the Southeast Pacific and Indonesia. In the Southeast Pacific, the water is normally rather cool. There is a permanent anticyclone, the Southeast Pacific anticyclone, to the west of South America. Over Indonesia a huge fountain of warm air rises above another permanent feature, the Indonesian low pressure area. (This is because the water in the western Pacific is much warmer, by between 7° to 12° C, than the water in the east.) At the surface of the ocean, between these two systems, easterly winds sweep across the Pacific.

## Sopping wet or dry as a bone?

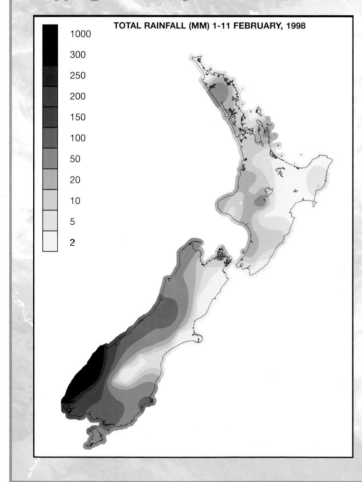

**TOTAL RAINFALL (MM) 1-11 FEBRUARY, 1998**

| 1000 |
| 300 |
| 250 |
| 200 |
| 150 |
| 100 |
| 50 |
| 20 |
| 10 |
| 5 |
| 2 |

The effect of mountains on the weather can be demonstrated by looking at the rainfall on either side of the main divide. The West Coast is wet, and the eastern coast is dry. An area just inland of the West Coast of the South Island has been nicknamed 'Godzone's Wet Zone', because its annual rainfall has been clocked at 10 metres! Compare this to the meagre yearly total of 30 centimetres which is recorded at arid Alexandra in Central Otago. Alexandra is only 65 kilometres to the east of the Wet Zone, but a world away on the dry side of the mountains. Even closer is Twizel, almost as dry as Alexandra but only 40 kilometres east of the Wet Zone.

*Typical rainfall distribution. Note the high rainfall totals in the west of the South Island and lower rainfall totals in the east of both islands, caused by the sheltering effects of the mountains when the westerly winds blow. (NIWA)*

The Southern Oscillation is the name of the tug of war between the Southeast Pacific anticyclone and the Indonesian fountain. The two players in the tug of war are called El Niño and La Niña. They each have very different effects on New Zealand.

New Zealand lies just to the south of all the action going on in the Southwest Pacific, but its climate is ultimately connected with it. Northern New Zealand protrudes into the subtropical anticyclonic belt, while the south of the country is very much embedded in the Roaring Forties of the mid-latitude belt. This, and the fact that New Zealand is located in the oceanic hemisphere, is why this country is open to many climate extremes. Although Britain is known for its changeable climate, it hardly rates compared to the extremes and changeability of our climate, created by our position in the southern weather machine, and the tug of war going on across the tropical Pacific. It is easy to see how New Zealand is vulnerable to a myriad of weather patterns and systems leading to climate hazards.

Another feature of the New Zealand landmass exaggerates these extremes. Aotearoa, the 'land of the long white cloud', is long and narrow, with a backbone of high mountains. Our mountain ranges are aligned south-west to north-east, and the gaps in the picket-fence created by Cook and Foveaux Straits dramatically modify weather systems when they arrive from the west. The mountains lift up any moist air flowing on to the land, which greatly accentuates any heavy rainfall, and the result is a deluge, rather than a shower, falling on the western side of the watershed. But the mountains shelter those areas downstream of the air flow, which causes droughts on the eastern side of the ranges.

The gaps between the islands and the gaps between the mountains also form natural wind funnels which the prevailing westerly winds accelerate through – as any Wellingtonian can tell you! Our mountains, mountain passes, and straits all act on the flow of air to produce our many climate extremes.

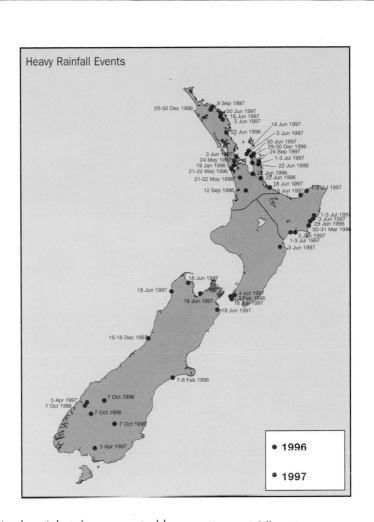

Heavy Rainfall Events

29-30 Dec 1996
9 Sep 1997
30 Jun 1997
18 Jun 1997
3 Jun 1997
18 Jun 1997
22 Jun 1996
3 Jun 1997
30 Jun 1997
29-30 Dec 1996
24 Sep 1997
3 Jun 1997
24 May 1997
1-3 Jul 1997
19 Jan 1996
22 Jun 1996
21-22 May 1996
22 Jun 1996
21-22 May 1996
22 Jun 1996
18 Jun 1997
12 Sep 1996
3 Jun 1997
1-3 Jul 1997
1-3 Jul 1997
3 Jun 1997
28 Jan 1996
30-31 Mar 1996
3 Jun 1997
1-3 Jul 1997
3 Jun 1997
18 Jun 1997
18 Jun 1997
4 oct 1997
7 Feb 1996
18 Jun 1997
18 Jun 1997
18 Jun 1997
15-16 Dec 1997
7-8 Feb 1996
5 Apr 1997
7 Oct 1996
7 Oct 1996
7 Oct 1996
7 Oct 1996
5 Apr 1997

• 1996
• 1997

*Heavy rainfall events 1996-1997.*
(NIWA)

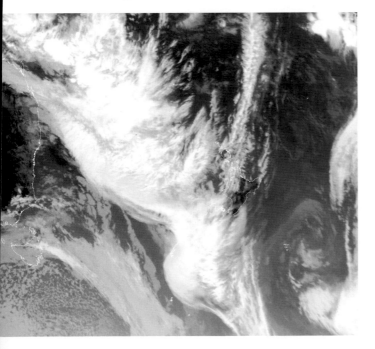

*Aotearoa, land of the long white cloud.*
(GMS-5 Weather Satellite/ JMA, courtesy of Victoria University)

*Dunedin airport at Momona, under water during the flooding of the Taieri Plains in 1979. (Otago Daily Times)*

## Send it down! heavy rainfall and floods

Heavy rain which causes floods has affected New Zealanders, and their use of the land, ever since there have been people living here. When heavy rain in 1840 caused the Hutt River to flood, the first Pākehā settlers were forced to move their settlement from Petone to Wellington. Last century Blenheim was nicknamed 'Beaver Town' because of the many floods it suffered at the mercy of the Wairau River. The devastation and loss of life caused by flooding cannot be over-estimated. There were 1115 recorded drownings up to 1870, and drowning was known as 'the New Zealand death'.

Climate figures and economic statistics from this century show that this reputation still stands. During 1996 and 1997 there were 23 significant episodes of flood-producing heavy rains. New Zealanders spent over $1 billion (in 1984 dollars) in the period 1951-1984 trying to prevent or repair damage caused by floods.

What makes New Zealand such a dangerously watery place to live? The two main causes of these destructive deluges are cyclones from the tropics, which bring a lot of rain to the northern part of the country, and wet air streams in 'troughs', which rise up over the mountains and hills and drop heavily on the land beneath.

*Cyclone Gavin approaching New Zealand. It affected New Zealand on 11 and 12 March 1997.*
*(GMS-5 Weather Satellite/ JMA, courtesy of Victoria University)*

## Wild cyclones from the tropics

Of all the storms that smite New Zealand, cyclones from the tropics do the most damage. They start in the tropics as warm air spinning vigorously in a spiral, inwards and upwards. The moisture-laden warm air produces heavy rainfall. But it is so intense that it creates a gale blowing around it. By the time a cyclone reaches these shores it has lost its warm core of air in the middle, but it can still

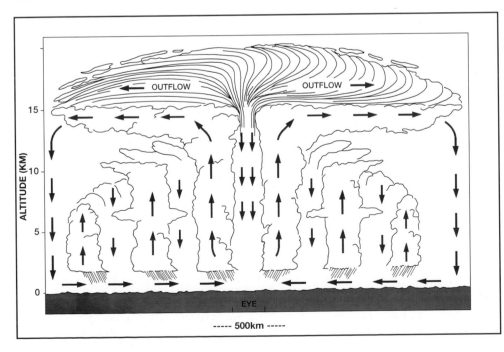

*Wind, rain, and airflow in a mature cyclone from the tropics.*
*(NIWA)*

*Sheep seek higher ground as a rail bridge across the Waipaoa River collapses during cyclone Bola, 1988.*
(Gisborne District Council).

Left: *A year's crop lost: kiwifruit vines spoiled by Cyclone Bola.*
(Gisborne Herald)

Right: *Tolaga Bay farmer Bruce Jeffers counts his losses after Cyclone Bola.*
(New Zealand Herald)

cause widespread devastation wherever its winds and rain make landfall.

Cyclone Bola was the most destructive cyclone to reach New Zealand in the twentieth century. Although it will be remembered for the flooding it caused on the East Coast of the North Island, its high winds cut a swath of damage through much of northern New Zealand.

Cyclone Bola started life in the South Pacific between Vanuatu and Fiji, and moved quite quickly to lie north of New Zealand by 6 March 1988. On 7 March it lay east of North Cape, then was diverted westwards on 8 and 9 March, to lie west of North Cape. During this three day period Cyclone Bola dragged in warm moist air from the east on to the East Coast from Napier to East Cape. Although cyclones contain moist air which produces heavy rain, Bola's position and continual driving of the wet air on to the ranges of Gisborne and Hawke's Bay brought another rain-inducing mechanism into play. When air is forced to rise over hills, it expands and becomes cooler, causing very heavy rainfall. In Bola's case, wet easterly winds blew against the East Coast ranges for three days, bringing huge amounts of rain. Over this period almost a metre of rain fell in the Gisborne Ranges, with over half a metre of rainfall in the hill country from Wairoa north. An average of 5000 tonnes of rain fell on every hectare of country!

Cyclone Bola will go down as the storm of the century. It produced a phenomenal amount of destruction over a wide area. The most visible evidence of Bola was the scarring of the East Coast landscape, still visible ten years later. The heavy rain washed away some of the most easily eroded land in New Zealand, leaving half the area pockmarked and scarred. The mud and soil washed down by the rivers in turn inundated the fertile cropping and horticultural land in the river valleys, damaged houses, and destroyed stopbanks, bridges, and roads. The damage to farms came to $18 million, due to stock losses and loss of land, while the flood damage to kiwifruit farms, vineyards, citrus orchards, and other crops on the floodplains totalled $15 million. Damage to roads and bridges was very extensive, with 40 per cent of the bridges in the area needing repairs. The bill to repair roads and bridges came to $34 million. The Waipaoa River, near Gisborne, brought down 33 million tonnes of soil and rock. The water supply to Gisborne City was cut, and the cost of putting this right was $11 million alone. Some 250 houses were flooded, and Gisborne Harbour was silted up. All up, the disaster relief bill came to $111 million. The effect of Cyclone Bola was to wash the mountains down to the plains and sea. It was not only the most destructive cyclone from the tropics of the century, but easily the most expensive.

## Troughs and fronts

When the weather forecast includes the words '...and a trough of low pressure...' you can expect rain to follow. Troughs are a bit like cake mixers combining a batter of air. They produce rain because they mix warmer moist air with cooler drier air and lift it up high. (Usually the warmer air contains tonnes of moisture, which then falls as rain.) A 'front' is the line along which the cold air meets the warm air.

This simple scenario can have pretty devastating consequences, however. People who were living in the Wellington area in the mid 1970s still vividly remember the floods just before Christmas in 1976. On 20 December, warm wet air blowing from the north met cooler air blowing from the south. This formed a line of rising air stretching from the hill suburbs of Wellington City, through Johnsonville, and up the western side of the Hutt Valley as far as Stokes Valley, Pinehaven, and Upper Hutt.

The result was a devastating zone of very vigorous rising air which created extremely heavy rain over Wellington and the Hutt Valley. The trough remained virtually stationary over the Wellington area for about 12 hours. There were deluges of more than 200 millimetres of rain in a 12 hour period in the region

*A detail from photograph below right, showing the power of the flood waters.*
(Evening Post)

*Below left: The flooded streets of Alicetown in 1976, with the Hutt River in the background.*
(Evening Post)

*Below right: The Petone overbridge during the 1976 floods.*
(Evening Post)

between Karori in the south and Whiteman's Valley, in Upper Hutt. The heaviest rainfall clocked up was 350 millimetres falling on the western hills of the Hutt Valley. The heaviest deluges that fell have been estimated to occur only about twice in a thousand-year period!

The heavy rains paralysed the whole Wellington region for the day. Wellington and the Hutt Valley were cut off from the rest of New Zealand, apart from Wellington Airport, which remained open for the entire day. Floodwaters and slips demolished many houses in the suburbs of Pinehaven and Stokes Valley, and also destroyed some houses near Petone. Flooding and rubble cut the road and railway line into the Hutt Valley, and silted up factories in Petone. Highway One, Wellington's main road link north, was also cut just north of the city. In central Wellington, there were floodwaters 30 centimetres deep on Lambton Quay. Fortunately, in spite of all the damage, there was only one person killed – when a landslip crushed a building. The Earthquake Commission (known as EQC) estimated the total damage to be $30 million.

## The demon drought

Drought has affected the New Zealand landscape many times in our history. One big nineteenth-century drought occurred in one of the most unlikely places in the whole country: the wet West Coast (where, in an average year, two and a half metres of rain falls). In February 1867 the rivers were so dry that gold miners were forced to stockpile dirt until the West Coast creeks flowed again, and the miners had enough water to sluice and pan for gold!

It is hard to imagine how drought could occur in this land of damp islands immersed in a huge ocean. But the cogs of the Southern Hemisphere weather machine do get stuck at times, and droughts may result.

*Marlborough farmer Joe Ferraby investigates one of the dried up dams on his property during the 1997/98 drought. Note the dead eel in the background!*
*(Terry Brosnahan, courtesy of Straight Furrow)*

Eel

Droughts have disrupted New Zealand life at various times over the past two hundred years. They are the most expensive climate disasters to smite this land. The twentieth century has seen ten major droughts so far. Parts of the country (especially inland Marlborough and Hawkes Bay) are currently suffering from drought as I write this chapter, though the drought will almost certainly have finished by the time you read it.

Droughts are very insidious. They are like no other hazard. They creep up gradually on a region. No one really notices as the soil dries out for lack of rain, the creeks dry up, and water reservoirs fall. Only when water supplies have become dangerously low, when it is often too late to do anything about it, do people suddenly wake up to what is happening. The most stressful aspect, once a drought has gripped the land, is the uncertainty about when it will end. Some droughts last only three or four months, but others have been known to last as long as ten months. The most devastating ones begin in spring, intensify in summer and last until the end of autumn. They often end dramatically when a deluge floods the drought-ravaged landscape.

The main culprit in the weather machine that causes droughts is the friendly weather system that brings fine weather and light winds – the 'high' or 'anticyclone'. These weather systems are made up of air gently spinning anticlockwise. Since the air is quietly descending, the sinking air is dry. This produces settled weather, light winds and, often, clear skies. Drought occurs in New Zealand when the weather machine gets stuck, with many slow moving anticyclones over New Zealand.

When the highs get stuck to the west of the North Island, particularly over summer, droughts occur in northern and western parts of the North Island and north of the South Island. In Gisborne and Hawke's Bay, droughts more commonly occur when the highs get stuck in the Tasman Sea, or north of New Zealand, and the westerlies of the Roaring Forties blow strongly over New Zealand, particularly in spring. Even other areas of Canterbury and Otago get afflicted by drought, but it occurs more often in winter and early spring when slow moving highs park themselves to the east of southern New Zealand.

One of the most devastating droughts occurred over a ten-month period from July 1988 to April 1989 on the east coast of the South Island. During this time little more than half the usual rainfall fell in South Canterbury and North Otago – about 25 to 35 centimetres of rain, which is about the annual total in the driest part of Central Otago. Quite often a drought is made worse by strong north-westerly winds, which tend to suck up any remaining water from the land. In some months of the drought, especially October 1988, there were frequent strong drying north-westerlies.

The drought devastated all the farms in South Canterbury and North Otago from the coast to the foothills. It was most severe in spring, when farmers had to send livestock to the freezing works early, or were forced to truck their stock to Nelson and Southland for grazing. A huge number of farms were affected – some 5,500 in all. On some farms stock numbers collapsed, with sheep and cattle numbers plummeting to a mere 5 per cent of normal levels. For the region as a whole, livestock numbers dropped by half. The drought also affected other farming

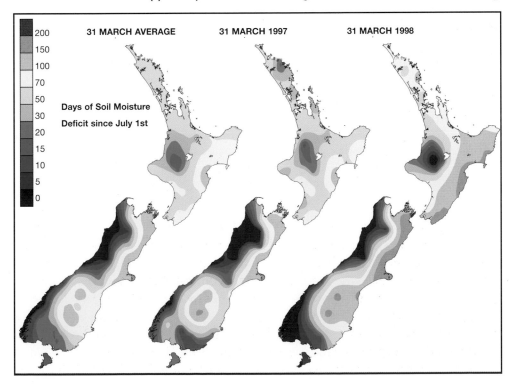

*Days of drought in the nine months to the end of March 1998. Note the high number of drought days, compared with the previous year, in areas affected by the 1997/98 El Niño-induced drought. (NIWA)*

*Heavy snowfall in Christchurch in 1992.*

(The Press, Christchurch)

activities, with only a quarter of the usual wheat being harvested. Financially it pushed some farmers to the wall, and they walked off their land.

Droughts such as these have knock-on effects. The devastation to sheep and cattle leaves remaining farm animals very weak. The following spring, many fewer lambs and calves were born than usual. The financial toll was huge: $200 million of lost farm income. This had a knock-on effect on the communities of Canterbury and North Otago, bringing the total cost somewhere near $400 million, with 11,000 farm jobs gone or at risk. The total costs of the 1997/98 El Niño and 1998/99 La Niña droughts have been estimated at $3-4 million!

## Deep and crisp and even

Exceptionally heavy snowfalls have blitzed New Zealand during winter and spring long before Pākehā settlement, and have caused much loss of life. Particularly harsh were the snowstorms during the early days of gold-mining in Central Otago.

*The year 1863 may be described as the year of rushes, floods and storms... . About the middle of July 1863 old Winter arose and smote the province with his mighty blast. First came snow, then warm heavy rain, which caused the snow on the mountains to melt suddenly; then all at once without further warning every river became flooded... . The Molyneux rose twenty feet in one night... . Just as the rains eased off and the community began to recover from the floods there was a tremendous fall of snow all over Otago. The whole country between Outram and the Lakes lay under a thick mantle of snow, the roads became invisible... .*

Gilkison, Early Days in Central Otago (1936)

Although the impacts of these storms have been less in dollar terms, they are the climate hazard that tends to cause loss of life to New Zealand's inhabitants, both human and animals alike. However, heavy snowfalls have been on the wane this century. There were nine exceptional falls in the second half of the nineteenth century, ten in the first half of the twentieth century, but only four in the latter part of the twentieth century (with a couple of winters still to go). Exceptional snowfalls usually only affect Canterbury, Otago, and Southland.

There are two causes of these: lows, in which a layer of higher-level warm air rides up over very cold air; and commando raids of very cold air sweeping up the east coast of the South Island.

Of the two, the lows produce much more widespread heavy snowfalls. Moist but very cold air from the sub-antarctic is drawn at low levels on to the east of the South Island. This air is forced to rise over the Canterbury, Otago, and Southland plains and hill country, but it is trapped from going any further by the higher Southern Alps. The low brings warm air into this cocktail from over the Southern Alps. This warm air overruns the cold air, the resulting cocktail producing the heavy snow. The snow usually falls most heavily under the areas where the very cold air is mixed up against the warmer air higher up.

The other type of heavy snowfall is produced when commando raids of cold air are drawn up in small vortices which attack the east of the South Island. These chilly charges have been known to get as far as the Wairarapa and Hawke's Bay on rare occasions.

A vigorous low brought the big snow of August 1992. This low crossed from Buller through Cook Strait to lie east of Canterbury from 26 to 29 August, bringing the heaviest snowfalls to the eastern South Island since 1939. Christchurch City had snow to a depth of 25 centimetres, and the snow lay around for three days. Higher up on the Canterbury Plains depths of half a metre were common, with snow drifts of more than a metre in the higher country. There were snowdrifts of up to six metres on Banks Peninsula! This storm brought widespread snow along the entire east of the South Island to sea level.

The snowstorm created havoc in the South Island. It brought down power lines, closed airports, roads and schools, and killed a million new-born lambs. Canterbury had stock deaths, power blackouts, and widespread school and road closures. Timaru and Dunedin Airports were closed, with many roads closed in inland Canterbury, Banks Peninsula, and Central Otago. The impact of the storm on farmers and their stock was particularly bad, as it hit at the peak of the lambing season. Many of the 6000 Canterbury farmers affected by snow lost 60 per cent of their lambs – a million lambs died, worth at least $40 million. Television and radio services were also cut throughout Canterbury. The melting snow also caused slips on the Port Hills, with the weight of snow causing the collapse of house roofs, conservatories, and guttering.

Although severe snowfalls produce havoc at the time, their impact on the landscape is not as lasting as the effects of heavy rainfall or droughts.

# Great balls of ice

Severe hailstorms are much more localised in their nature, but wherever these strike they still cause damage and disruption. New Zealand gets its fair share of hail, and news reports throughout the century describe falls of hail the size, variously, of tennis balls, golf balls, cricket balls, pigeon eggs, pennies, and walnuts.

These more localised affairs have a preference for the South Island east coast from Oamaru to Rangiora, although no part of New Zealand is completely free of attack. Hail is usually caused by thunderstorms. Thunderstorms contain warm rising air. These updrafts of warm rising air are caused either by fronts, which provide a lift to the air, or are triggered by the heating of air over land. Once this updraft of warmer air develops, water droplets form, and as the initial rain and hail drops, it forms a downdraft. Large hail falls out of thunderstorms which have strong updrafts and downdrafts. What happens is the initial small hailstone gets caught in the updraft, and collides with other ice and water particles as it rises. The growing hailstones whirl around in these thunderstorms until they get too big and heavy, when they drop to the ground.

In New Zealand, hailstorms are considered severe when hail is half a centimetre in diameter (pea size) or larger, because hail of this size damages crops and property. Hail causes more loss in dollars than other types of thunderstorm-spawned severe weather (such as tornadoes and localised deluges), mainly to crops but sometimes to buildings. The thunderstorms of the late spring of 1996 were such examples. Hailstorms occurred in the Wairarapa on 2 and 3 November, and in Hawke's Bay on 4 November. Then on 5 December a dramatic thunderstorm with severe hail hit parts of Canterbury. The hailstones were up to

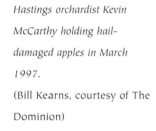

*Hastings orchardist Kevin McCarthy holding hail-damaged apples in March 1997.*

*(Bill Kearns, courtesy of The Dominion)*

the size of a 20 cent piece near Christchurch. The next day severe marble to golf-ball-sized hail struck Hawke's Bay. On 15 December further pea-sized hail occurred in the Nelson areas. All these hail-producing thunderstorms occurred in squall lines, often with south-westerly winds.

The series of hailstorms knocked holes in the national fruit crop, causing particular damage to apple growers. The early November hail strikes hit 28 Wairarapa orchards. Eight orchards had more than 65 per cent of their fruit damaged. About 75,000 export cartons of fruit were destroyed, worth about $1.8 million. The early December hailstorms caused large crop losses, particularly near Havelock North, where one in five orchards was struck. This resulted in millions of dollars worth of damage to the fruit and orchards. The final storm in December hit 120 orchards in the Motueka area. Of these, 10 orchards suffered 80 per cent damage to their crops. This hailstorm caused an estimated $20 million worth of damage to orchards.

## Blown away

New Zealand has been dubbed 'the windy isles' because of the way the storms and weather systems of the Roaring Forties and Furious Fifties batter the country. Compared with its antipodes, Spain, New Zealand is much windier; partly a consequence of visits of cyclones from the tropics but, more importantly, being immersed in the vigorous cogs of the Southern Hemisphere weather machine that whirl around the Southern Oceans. The blocking effect of the mountains helps to make the winds stronger, particularly through the wind gaps of Cook and Foveaux Straits and the Manawatu Gorge. The wind statistics reflect this. Wellington has 173 days per year of strong winds and Invercargill has 110 days, Palmerston North has 78 days, compared with only 60 days per year in sultry Auckland.

At high wind speeds, the constant gusting of the wind acts like a wrench on objects. Wind will tear off roofs, uproot trees, and blow power poles down. There are two main actors that bring particularly high winds: cyclones from the tropics, and strong nor'westers over the country. As described above, cyclones from the tropics are vigorous spinning-wheels of air. When they get near New Zealand they often change, and the injection of colder air into them accelerates them to produce severe gale-force winds. When these blow against the coast of New Zealand, or through one of the wind gaps in the mountain backbone, then extreme winds eventuate.

The nor'wester usually occurs before a cold front or a belt of rain associated with a wind change crosses the country. Particularly strong nor'westers are reasonably frequent, but violent nor'westers occur about once every twenty years. Normally the nor'wester is blocked on the West Coast by the Southern Alps, causing the north-westerly air either to leak through the mountains higher up, or to reach the ground east of the Alps from higher levels. However, occasionally the nor'westers get so strong that they are forced into waves by the mountain barriers. The waves gather speed on the other side of the mountains, usually in inland Canterbury. In rare cases they become so strong that north-westerly winds of great strength will batter all eastern areas from Southland to

*The ferry* Wahine *foundering in Wellington Harbour during the storm, 10 April 1968.* (Evening Post)

Gisborne, reaching well out to sea to the east.

The 'Wahine storm' on 10 April 1968 will go down in history as the windstorm of the century. A cyclone from the tropics was born in the Coral Sea on 5 April, and cruised south to lie off North Cape by 9 April. It then moved south-east, down to Tauranga, and finally headed out to sea just south of Napier to lie off the Wairarapa coast. It was lying east of Kaikoura by noon on 10 April. As it was crossing the North Island, the cyclone wound up in strength to create a maelstrom near Cook Strait, before travelling down the east coast of the South Island. During this phase, horrendous wind speeds were reached. Wind gusts peaked near 270 km/h at Oteranga Bay on the edge of Cook Strait. This is the highest wind speed to have ever been recorded in New Zealand. Wind speeds in Wellington were clocked at 200 km/h, and the wind was so violent that it destroyed the wind speed measuring instruments at Wellington Airport. No more intense storm is known to have battered areas of New Zealand. (Cyclone Bola was less intense, but its effects were more widely felt.)

The greatest destruction from the wind occurred around Wellington. Many hundreds of trees were uprooted, and roofs blown off houses. The most destructive feature of the windstorm was the disabling of the inter-island ferry *Wahine*. It ran aground on Barrett's Reef at the entrance to Wellington Harbour, and subsequently sank with the loss of 51 lives.

The most destructive nor'wester in history was the big blow on 1 August 1975. This storm was caused by extremely strong north-westerly winds preceding a cold front. The case is outstanding for two reasons: the extremely strong north-westerlies, and the widespread extent of severe winds, which blew from Southland to Gisborne. Peak wind gusts of 170 km/h were recorded near Dunedin, Timaru, and Christchurch. The most severe winds lasted about three hours. This windstorm created the usual havoc, uprooting trees, toppling power lines, and blowing roofs off buildings. In Canterbury the storm was outstanding for the widespread destruction in the four major state forests, as well as other smaller plantations. In Eyrewell, Ashley, Balmoral, and Hanmer forests combined, over 6000 hectares of trees were blown over: about a quarter of the trees planted. The amount of timber trees toppled in Canterbury was 2.2 million cubic metres. Fortunately, some of the timber could be salvaged.

*Eyrewell State Forest, Canterbury, blasted flat by severe north-west gales in August 1975. The inset shows that most trees were blown over at the roots!*
*(AAQA 6395, M11997 and M12019, National Archives, Wellington)*

## Aotearoa's changing climate

New Zealand's climate has changed a lot in the past, so there is no reason to expect it not to vary in the future, particularly with global warming going on. The fluctuations and changes in our climate have a large effect in modulating the climate extremes. The most famous actor causing changes from year to year is the Southern Oscillation tug of war between El Niño and La Niña. These two dramatically affect our weather and our climate.

## El Niño

El Niño means 'the boy child' in Spanish. The term was traditionally used by Peruvian anchovy fishermen, when warm seas occured around Christmas. An El Niño occurs when the fountain of rising air over Indonesia and the Southeast Pacific anticyclone are both weak. Water that is much warmer than usual floods into the eastern tropical Pacific Ocean, at the same time as the easterly winds in the tropics disappear. This phase of the Southern Oscillation is the world-famous El Niño – famous because it causes dramatic climate disruptions right around the globe.

Many New Zealanders dislike El Niño – especially those of us who live on the West Coast, Southland, and Otago. In an El Niño the westerly and south-westerly winds of the Roaring Forties rev up, especially in spring and summer. The weather

*Dust storm in the Awatere Valley. In the drier conditions typical of El Niños in Marlborough, dust storms like this will be more frequent. (Denis Eden, courtesy of Landcare Research)*

over all the country becomes cool and windy. Our climate records show that it is typically very cloudy and wet in the west and south of the South Island, while in other parts of the country conditions are dry and windy. In fact, Marlborough and eastern areas of the North Island go into drought. Although temperatures are slightly warmer in Gisborne and Hawke's Bay, the incessant westerly winds make conditions particularly dry.

The big El Niño of 1982-3 still lingers in the memories of many. During that summer, eastern areas from Canterbury to Gisborne were gripped by drought. People living in other North Island areas complained about the incessant wind, especially Wellingtonians. And perhaps the greatest complaints were voiced by southerners, who missed summer completely! There, and on the West Coast, frequent rain and cold south-west winds blew away any vestige of summer. Perhaps the most famous legacies of El Niños over New Zealand are drought. El Niño caused the drought of 1982-3 and was a factor in the 1992 South Island power crisis and

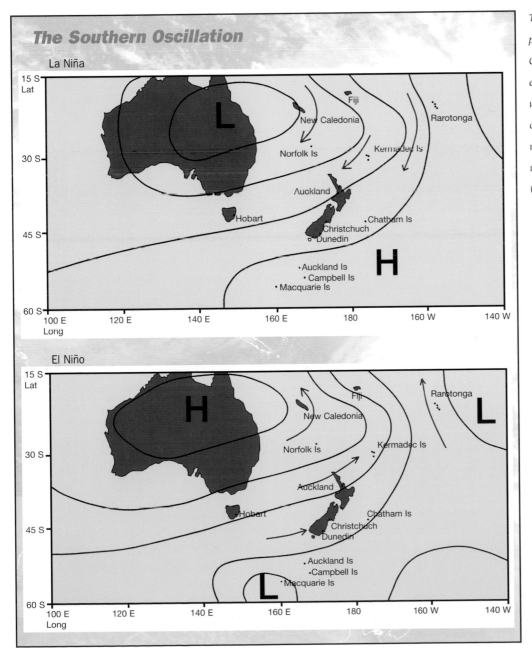

The El Niño and La Niña phases of the Southern Oscillation. During La Niñas, easterly and north-easterly winds and weather are more common. El Niños bring westerly and south-westerly winds and weather patterns. (NIWA)

Clouds and wind

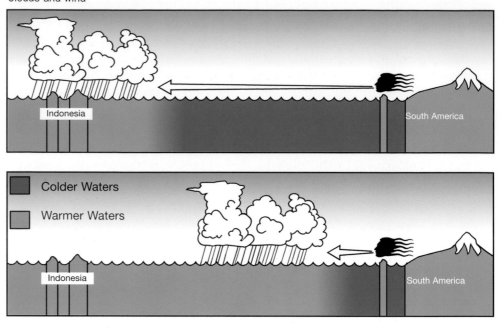

Colder Waters
Warmer Waters

the 1994 Auckland water crisis. El Niño caused the East Coast drought of 1994-5 and the Marlborough and North Canterbury droughts of 1994-5 and 1997-8.

## La Niña

If El Niño is on one side of the Southern Oscillation coin, the other face shows La Niña. When the tropical Pacific is in this phase, the fountain of rising air over Indonesia is very strong, and so too is the Southeast Pacific anticyclone. This makes the easterly winds sweeping across the tropical Pacific a lot stronger, with the water in the eastern tropical Pacific much colder than normal. The La Niña phase also disrupts climate patterns around the globe, but in a different way from El Niño.

Most residents of New Zealand like La Niña, except those living in the northern half of the North Island. In this phase the prevailing westerly winds that sweep

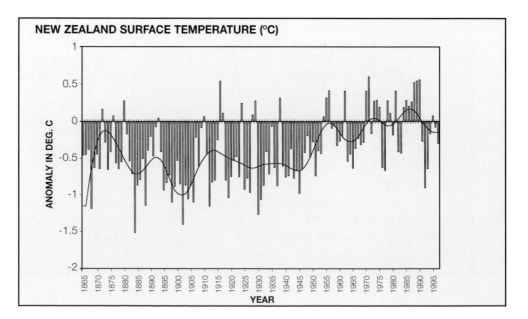

NEW ZEALAND SURFACE TEMPERATURE (°C)

## Icy blast!

In the chilly depths of the last Ice Age, about 20,000 to 25,000 years ago, New Zealand was subject to very much revved up westerly winds over the whole country. With temperatures 5° C down on the mid-twentieth century, temperatures in Auckland would have been similar to those recorded in Invercargill today. Temperatures were lower across the whole planet, and the chill created great ice sheets over Europe and North America. This tied lots of water up in the form of ice, and lowered the sea level to such an extent that New Zealand's three main islands were all joined into one landmass. You could have walked across what is now Cook Strait, or cycled from the present Waitemata Harbour right out to Great Barrier Island. Much of the Southern Alps and their foothills were filled with ice, and the West Coast glaciers pushed right out to sea. Westerly winds battered the landscape, producing severe snowstorms in the west of the South Island and in the ranges, with much more frequent westerly windstorms in Canterbury producing gales, high and low temperatures. Wellington would have been most unpleasant, with incessant northerly gales. The westerly blasts would have dried out the landscape in the north and east of both islands, and there would have been much more extensive drought than today. These windstorms were responsible for large deposits of windborne dust, called loess. The vegetation responded – grasslands filled all eastern areas from Marlborough to Southland.

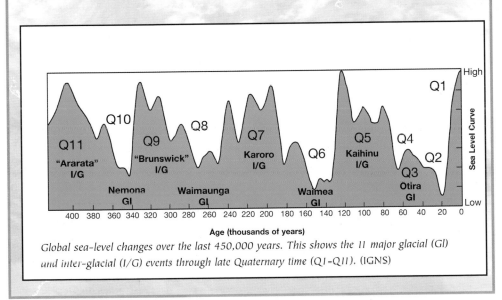

Global sea-level changes over the last 450,000 years. This shows the 11 major glacial (Gl) and inter-glacial (I/G) events through late Quaternary time (Q1-Q11). (IGNS)

over New Zealand become very much weaker, and north-easterly winds blow more often. The weather over the entire country is warm. In fact, all the warm years in our climate record occurred under La Niña conditions.

There is a downside, though. For those who live in the northern half of the North Island and Nelson the weather can be very cloudy and wet. Often there is much more heavy rain and flooding than usual in Northland, Auckland, the Bay of Plenty, and sometimes in Gisborne and Hawke's Bay. Nelson also gets it wet. Meanwhile, other parts of the country have dry sunny weather, especially the south west of the North Island and the South Island West Coast. The other disadvantage of La Niña years is that cyclones from the tropics often visit the north of New Zealand. When these occur, floods and windstorms can occur anywhere in northern New Zealand, and also in Gisborne and Hawke's Bay. A major La Niña happened in 1988-89, with another one occurring over the 1998-99 season, which produced a devastating drought in South Canterbury and eastern Otago.

*Flooding in Queenstown in 1878 due to high levels of Lake Wakatipu. (Burton Brothers Collection, Te Papa)*

## Climate through time

New Zealand's landscape has experienced large climate changes over the passage of time. In the depths of the last Ice Age, around 20,000 years ago, average temperatures were 5°C lower than they were in the middle of the twentieth century. It looks now as though global warming is likely to warm the region by 2°C by the year 2100. These climate changes have had dramatic impacts on the landscape and its inhabitants, particularly with changes in the incidence of floods, droughts, snow and windstorms. Those differences in average temperature may seem small, but they have a huge impact on the landscape and the lives of the creatures living there.

Last century, when the first European colonists arrived, the country was much colder than it is in the 1990s. New Zealand was experiencing the end of the Little Ice Age, a time of cooler climate right over the planet which lasted about 250 years. The first thermometer measurements taken in New Zealand in the 1850s and 1860s showed temperatures that were 1°C below those of the average temperatures of the 1990s.

Evidence of the cooler landscape and greater mantle of snow and ice in the mountains comes from the European explorers who mapped the glaciers. The observations of Julius von Haast in sketches, maps, and photographs were put on canvas by the paintings of John Gully. These show greatly expanded glaciers in the

Mt Cook region. Some of the glaciers, such as the Dart and the Godley, reached as much as 5 kilometres further down their valleys than they are now! They were also much thicker. Like the Tasman Glacier, which wasn't much longer than it is today, the Dart and the Godley were a full 100 metres thicker than they are currently. Temperatures in New Zealand showed little change right up to 1950, when the climate began to warm up.

The cooler period of climate was marked with extremes – particularly those associated with colder weather. Exceptional snowstorms were much more frequent, averaging 10 every 50 years, compared with four in the last 50 years. Icebergs were sighted in the New Zealand region in the 1850s and again in the 1890s. Floods and drought occurred, and the greatest El Niño of the nineteenth century, in 1878, produced dramatic extremes. The rainfall in the west of the South Island was double the annual average, whilst the east suffered from

*Franz Josef Glacier. These two images show the extent of glacier retreat since the late nineteenth century. The upper photograph was taken in the 1880s, and the lower one in the 1980s.*
(Muir and Moodie Collection, Te Papa; IGNS)

*Icebergs have been observed as far north as the Chatham Islands and were last seen in the 1950s. This is an artist's impression of the scene as viewed from just south of Waitangi, Chatham Island.*
(Hamish Campbell; Te Papa)

drought, as incessant westerly winds pounded New Zealand. It was so wet in the Southern Lakes that Lake Wakatipu rose to its highest level, and flooded Eicharts Hotel in lower Queenstown. Storms in September of 1878 generated the largest floods on record in the Clutha and Waitaki Rivers. However, in the east it was a different story. The year 1878 was the second driest on record in both Napier and Christchurch.

A shift in climate occurred in the 1950s, when climate warming occurred. Recorded temperatures over New Zealand warmed by between 0.5° C and 1° C. The warmer temperatures have had effects on our environment, perhaps the most noticeable of which is the marked loss of ice in all the South Island glaciers. Since 1950 the Franz Josef Glacier has retreated up its valley by more than a kilometre. By 1981 the Classen and Godley Glaciers had shrunk from their 1861 positions by five kilometres and three kilometres respectively. Climate warming has already caused some changes in crops grown in parts of New Zealand. It is now possible to grow wine grapes in Canterbury, while kiwifruit is now a less suitable crop to grow in Northland than it used to be.

The 1950s and 1960s were marked by alternating El Niño and La Niña events bringing floods and droughts. The number of winter and spring heavy snowfalls to affect the lower lands on Canterbury, Otago, and Southland has markedly decreased. During this period, the prevailing westerly and south-westerly winds over New Zealand have blown less strongly, and there have been more easterlies and north-easterlies.

The final change in New Zealand's twentieth century climate occurred in the mid 1970s, with an increase in El Niño events in the Pacific Ocean. There has been an immediate response over New Zealand in the strengthening of the westerly and south-westerly winds. However, temperatures have not dropped, as you might otherwise expect, because of global warming. The more frequent El Niños have caused the glaciers on the West Coast of the South Island to make small advances as they receive more snow. The El Niños have caused more floods and droughts, too – floods have become more frequent on the West Coast, and along the South Island rivers fed by rains from the west; while El Niño-induced droughts in the east of the North Island have become much more common. These droughts have sometimes extended their arid fingers into other northern and eastern areas of New Zealand.

## Next century's weather

Whether you're an apple grower in Napier-Hastings or Nelson, or a regional council planner in a coastal part of New Zealand, climate change is likely to play an increasingly large part in planning decisions over the next several decades and beyond. Climate scientists are quite clear that greenhouse gases in the atmosphere are increasing, and that these must have an impact on climate. There is incontrovertible evidence that amounts of greenhouse gases in the atmosphere started rising at the start of the industrial revolution, and are continuing to do so at an accelerating rate.

The greenhouse gases, carbon dioxide, methane, and CFCs, trap heat in the atmosphere. The basic laws of physics require that an increase in these gases will change climate. This is not just a conclusion arrived at by scientists in New Zealand. It is the considered opinion of the world's most respected climate scientists, who were asked by the United Nations in 1988 to report on how rising amounts of greenhouse gases in the atmosphere might change global climate. The conclusions of the first report of the Intergovernmental Panel on Climate Change (IPCC), a group of more than 200 top scientists from around the world, have not changed, despite intensive and continuing research and analysis. When the global climate system has fully adjusted to a doubling of greenhouse gases, we face a warming of between 1.5° C and 4.5° C. The most reliable estimate of the warming is an increase of 2° C by 2100.

While past climate changes have had huge effects on the weather, and on life and land in New Zealand, it is impossible to say with any certainty what effects will be in every region in the world, particularly because the change will happen much more quickly than ever before. The approach scientists use to deal with these uncertainties is to develop 'scenarios' that describe a plausible range of future climates for a region, consistent with the latest climate modelling results.

The latest scenarios for New Zealand suggest that by 2030 inland areas of Canterbury and Otago may have warmed by 0.5 to 2° C, with a temperature rise of 0.5 to 1.5° C everywhere else. The scenarios also suggest that throughout most of New Zealand there will be more rain, and the rainfall will be heavier – apart from Wellington and North Canterbury, which could be drier in winter and spring. It is also likely that the difference between daytime and night-time temperatures could be smaller in areas that become cloudier. Observations already support this particular part of the scenario: in the western half of the North Island there has been a measured reduction in the difference between day and night temperatures in recent decades, with fewer frosts.

*How Canterbury may look in a warmer twenty-first century!*
*(Brian Enting and Michael Pole – Key-Light)*

Then there is the range of effects on New Zealand's agricultural, horticultural, forestry, fishing, and electricity industries, to name but a few. Crops will grow differently in a warmer world. Many regions will find that their current crops and pasture species are no longer suitable under a changed climate. Research completed recently by NIWA, the National Institute of Water and Atmospheric Research, shows that if temperatures rise by 2 to 3° C, the climate in the major apple areas of Hawke's Bay and Nelson would be unsuitable for growing apples. Instead, Central Otago, Wairarapa, Canterbury, and parts of Marlborough would become prime apple-growing areas.

Native forests are expected to be hit hard by the changing climate. The Greenhouse 94 Conference held in Wellington in October 1994 heard that temperatures will rise too fast for many species such as kauri and puriri. They will be unable to adjust quickly enough to establish themselves in more suitable climates several hundred kilometres away, and without human intervention there is a high chance they will become extinct.

On a brighter note, warmer temperatures are likely to mean more snapper in coastal waters around New Zealand, because when sea temperatures are warmer,

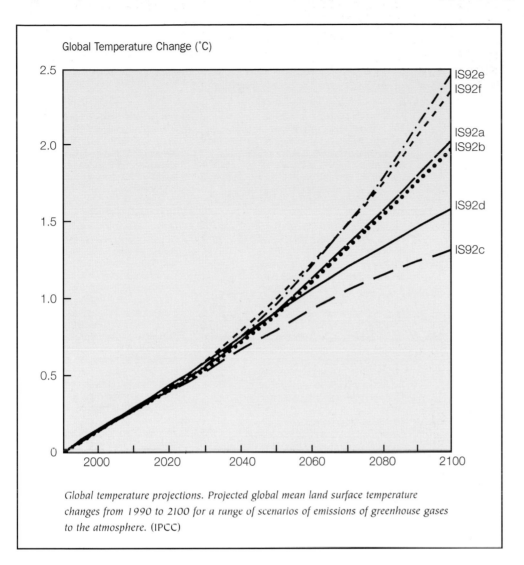

Global Temperature Change (°C)

2.5 — IS92e
      IS92f

2.0 — IS92a
      IS92b

1.5 — IS92d

1.0

0.5 — IS92c

0

2000   2020   2040   2060   2080   2100

*Global temperature projections. Projected global mean land surface temperature changes from 1990 to 2100 for a range of scenarios of emissions of greenhouse gases to the atmosphere. (IPCC)*

greater numbers of juvenile snapper survive their first five months. Climate change is also expected to bring a reduction to New Zealand's electricity requirements in winter, while at the same time the extra snow melting under warmer temperatures will put more water in the South Island's hydro storage lakes. Associate Professor Blair Fitzharris from Otago University told the Greenhouse 94 Conference that by 2020 climate change could be responsible for a 12 to 16 per cent increase in electricity generation, and a 6 to 10 per cent drop in consumption.

These scenarios of possible future conditions in parts of New Zealand describe what is likely to happen in the next few decades. They will be refined as the full extent of global warming begins to show up in the observations we make of the changes in our climate.

The change in climate forces created by warming will change the pattern of climate extremes. Warmer air holds more moisture, which means that heavy rainfall and floods are more likely. If the present trend to more El Niños continues, then droughts in the north and east will become more common. However, the jury is still out on this trend! The trend to less heavy snowfalls seems likely, unless there are more large explosive volcanic eruptions like that of Mt Pinatubo in the Philippines, which would push a dust veil into the atmosphere to cool the climate for a year or two. Volcanic eruptions are largely unpredictable, though the patterns of climate change are becoming easier to predict.

# Major weather events

Records of early severe weather events in New Zealand are sketchy, and in preparing a historical list of floods, droughts, and snow and wind storms it is difficult to rate the records of events in any order of importance. The following lists of significant weather events have been compiled from such records that are available. The list is of selected events and is not exhaustive.

## Floods

| | |
|---|---|
| 1863 | Over 100 lives lost during a 6-week period in July-August. Major flooding of Clutha and tributaries. |
| 1945 | 20-22 February. South Canterbury. £485,000 damage. 20-21 May. Canterbury, particularly Christchurch, with 320 mm rain in 3 days at Akaroa. |
| 1968 | 8-9 March. Dunedin, coastal north Otago, and South Canterbury. April. *Wahine* Storm. Northland, Auckland, Bay of Plenty (9-10 April), Christchurch/Banks Peninsula (10-11 April) and Southland/west Otago (15 April). |
| 1971 | 24 February. New Plymouth. Stratford Mountain House had a two-day (24-25 February) rainfall of 795 mm, one of the highest two-day rainfalls ever recorded in New Zealand. |
| 1976 | 20-21 December. Hutt Valley. Damage estimated at $30 million. |
| 1984 | 26-27 January. Southland. $46 million in damages. |
| 1986 | 2-13 March. Southern Canterbury/northern Otago. $60 million damages. |
| 1988 | 5-9 March. Cyclone Bola devastated Gisborne area. Extensive flooding and damage estimated at $73 million. |
| 1990 | 9 March. Taranaki/Wanganui. Ex tropical cyclone Hilda caused severe flooding. At least 700 sheep died. Rainfall of 338 mm in 24 hours at Lepperton. |
| 1994 | 21-22 January Westland/Fiordland/Southern Lakes. Slips and flooding; roads and bridges washed out. Rainfall totalled 682 mm in 24 hours at Colliers Creek, Westland, a new New Zealand record; 538 mm at Milford Sound. |
| 1995 | 29 March. Northland. A 100 year event, with extraordinary high rainfall, thunderstorms, and severe flooding in the Whangarei/Hikurangi area. Rainfall totalled 218 mm in 6 hours (a 100-year event) and over 300 mm in 24 hours. |

## Droughts

| | |
|---|---|
| 1916-17 | Summer. Between November and March. Severe at Wanganui, Nelson, and parts of Marlborough. 58 consecutive days without rain at Farewell Spit, 17 mm in 75 days at Wanganui. |
| 1919 | Summer-autumn. Two dry periods commencing in February and April. Most severe in parts of South Canterbury, North Otago, Bay of Plenty, and Taupo. 14 mm in 65 days at Oamaru. |
| 1938-39 | Summer. Commenced in December and was broken by rain in April. Severe in parts of Auckland, Nelson, and Marlborough provinces. The driest March on record in some places. |
| 1945-46 | Summer. Severe in parts of north Auckland and Hawke's Bay. No rain for 34 consecutive days at Taupo and Napier. 28 mm in 122 days at Napier. |
| 1956 | Summer. Worst drought in Canterbury's history, and serious in Otago. |
| 1958-59 | September to March. Drought became very serious over most of New Zealand by October. |
| 1978 | January to March. One of the most severe droughts that has ever been experienced in New Zealand. Most severe in much of the North Island, Nelson, Marlborough, and South Canterbury. |
| 1988-89 | March 1988 to April 1989. Major drought affected east coast of South Island. Worst affected areas were initially South Canterbury/North Otago, but as the drought spread north, north Canterbury became the worst affected area. |
| 1991 | March-July. West Coast/Southern Lakes. By July, waters in South Island hydro-lakes had reached their lowest levels since the 1950s. |
| 1994 | March-July. Auckland. A very extended period of low rainfall persisted in Auckland, resulting in water restrictions in June (normally a wet month). Unusually high rainfall relieved the crisis in July. |
| 1997-99 | December 1997-May 1998. Eastern New Zealand. Summer rainfall in these areas was unusually low, and for some places the lowest ever measured in their historical record. Severe drought became re-established in Canterbury by the end of the year, spreading into North and east Otago, and Southland during early 1999. |

## Snowstorms

| | |
|---|---|
| 1863 | Canterbury/Otago. First unusually heavy snowfall reported by colonists. |
| 1867 | Canterbury/Otago. Most severe snowfall on record at the time. |
| 1878 | Canterbury/Otago. June. 107 cm at Bealey (Canterbury), with up to 4.5 m at Arthur's Pass and 7.5 cm at Christchurch. |
| 1895 | Canterbury/Otago. Very cold over much of South Island and Southland from April to September. Up to 90 cm of hard-packed frozen snow in many areas. Worst snowfall on record at the time. |
| 1903 | Canterbury/Otago. Snow lay for 5 weeks in many areas. 45 cm at Ashburton |
| 1939 | Canterbury/Otago/Southland. July and August. Affected Otago and Southland, giving Dunedin City its worst snowfall ever. Central and South Canterbury received a heavy fall in September. |
| 1945 | Canterbury. July, a very heavy snowfall down to coastal areas. 30 cm about Christchurch, Ashburton and Timaru. Similar to 1903 and as bad as 1895 in some places. |
| 1967 | Central North Island and South Island. 16-18 November. Worst in Mackenzie Country. 60-70,000 sheep killed. |
| 1973 | Canterbury/Northern Otago. 5-6 August. Heaviest since July 1945. 100,000 sheep and 3000 cattle killed. Extensive disruption of communications, power supply, and transport. |
| 1992 | 16-23 June. Otago/Southland. Heavy snowfall to inland and high country areas, and record low day and night time temperatures. Snow lay at Queenstown for the remainder of the month. 27-29 August. South Island East Coast. Widespread snow to sea level along the entire east coast of the South Island. The most severe snowstorm to affect Christchurch since 14 July 1945. |
| 1995 | 2-4 June. Hundalees. Otago/Inland south Canterbury. Snow 40 cm deep at Arthur's Pass, and 20-25 cm deep (with drifts up to 70 cm) in the Queenstown/Wakatipu area. 14-18 July. Eastern New Zealand. Widespread snowfall to sea level on 16 July from Wellington to Gisborne, lying for the first time in living memory at Rotorua. 25 September. Southland/Otago/South Canterbury. 50,000 lambs lost in high country areas. |
| 1996 | 1-4 July. Southland/Otago/Canterbury and Napier-Taupo Road. Heavy snowfall up to 30 cm deep in Southland and Otago on 1 and 2 July, followed by record low temperatures. Snowfall 15 cm deep at Ashburton. Napier-Taupo road snow to 35 cm deep, the worst for 40 years. |

## Windstorms

| | |
|---|---|
| 1945 | 13 July. Storm-force nor'westers in Canterbury severely damaged 1400 ha of Balmoral Forest. |
| 1964 | 22 March. Storm-force nor'westers in Canterbury destroyed 4050 ha of Eyrewell Forest. |
| 1968 | 10 April. Cyclone Giselle caused peak gusts of 145 knots near Wellington, leading to the sinking of the inter-island ferry *Wahine*. Total losses due to storm estimated at $14 million. |
| 1975 | 1 August. Severe nor'westers destroyed 6000 ha of Canterbury forests, damaged buildings and uprooted trees throughout Canterbury, Otago and Southland. Wind gusts exceeded 90 knots in many areas. Losses in Canterbury estimated at $7 million. |

Our country comprises a few islands straddling the boundary between two of the Earth's massive, moving tectonic plates. New Zealand is a land in motion. That means we are prone to all sorts of life-threatening and property-destroying natural disasters.

Luckily, there are things that you and your family can do to protect people, property, and possessions.

## Minimising damage

Here are some of the ways you and your family can prevent or minimise damage to your property – **and reduce the risk to personal safety.**

- Make sure your house is securely connected to the piles with bolts or nail plates. Use metal bands to secure chimneys. Securely tie hot water cylinders and header tanks to ensure they don't topple. (A qualified builder will be able to help with all of these.)
- Screw or wire back tall furniture to the wall framing.
- On open shelves, store heavy items low down, or put them in cupboards.
- Good cupboard latches, plastic putty under ornaments, velcro pads under TVs, stereos, and other electronic appliances, and closing picture hooks after hanging items on them can all make a big difference.
- Get professional advice about what to do with unstable slopes.
- In coastal areas, tsunami can be a threat. Keep property well above the high-tide mark and make sure it is well secured.

## Know what to do

Consult the inside back cover of the Yellow Pages for handy tips on what to do in the event of disasters such as earthquake, tsunami, volcanic eruption, storm, fire, and flooding. Make sure you have a working radio at all times. This may be your only source of information and advice until help arrives.

In a disaster, you may be on your own for the first three days. Are you prepared? Do you have emergency supplies (water, food, fuel, batteries, blankets, medical supplies) to last three days? Do all family members know how and when to turn off water, gas and electricity at the main switches? Does each member of your household know what to do, and how to communicate with each other if they become stranded away from the home? Have you determined the best escape routes from your home for each kind of disaster? Where are the safe spots in your home for each type of disaster?

- If you have to evacuate, take essential medicines, toilet items, baby needs, important documents, radio, torch, extra clothing and footwear. Consider your neighbours, your pets and animals. Turn off all utilities and secure your premises.
- In an earthquake, keep calm, stay indoors, and take cover. After the shaking has stopped, check yourselves and your neighbours for injuries and treat;

turn off heaters, water, electricity, gas, and heating oil at the mains. Keep alert for aftershocks.

- In a flood, raise or remove valuables and poisonous chemicals. Avoid flooded areas.
- In a tsunami, move inland to high ground. Never go to the coast, and avoid streams and rivers.
- In a volcanic eruption, stay indoors, and close doors and windows. If you have to go outside, wear substantial clothing, carry a torch, and breathe through a cloth.

## Insuring against damage

Sometimes natural disasters can be so powerful that doing everything you can to minimise or prevent damage is not enough. That's why insurance is important.

**EQC is New Zealand's natural-disaster insurer for residential property.** You get EQC natural disaster insurance automatically when you buy insurance for your home or its contents from a private insurance company. Your home is then insured for replacement value up to $100,000 plus GST and your contents for up to $20,000 plus GST. For property with values above these, most insurance companies offer top-up cover (extra cover up to full replacement value). EQC covers you against earthquake, landslip, volcanic eruption, hydrothermal activity, and tsunami. For details of EQCover and top-up cover, contact your private insurer.

## After a disaster

**Personal safety is the priority. Remember to listen to the radio for important messages.** If you have property damage you may

- clean up, dispose of, or move things, but take photos first if you can
- make temporary repairs for safety or to prevent further damage or discomfort
- repair, or get repaired, essential services such as toilets, but keep everything that is replaced and a copy of the bill
- clean up spillages and breakages, but don't throw anything away unless it is perishable
- dispose of perishables such as food from a broken freezer, but make a list of the items first.

**There are also a number of things you must do, including**

- taking reasonable steps to protect your property and prevent more damage (such as turning off the gas and boarding up broken windows)
- not starting any non-essential repairs without EQC approval
- letting someone from EQC come on to your property to inspect the damage.

You can get more information about EQC insurance and what to do after a disaster from EQC's *Householder's Guide to EQCover*, available from EQC or your private insurer.

**For EQCover claims ring toll free on 0800 652 333.** For more information ring toll free 0800 652 333; write to EQC, PO Box 311, Wellington; visit website http://www.eqc.govt.nz, or contact your private insurance company.

# Index

Note: Page numbers in **bold** refer to illustrations.